T0179350

Programming Media
Art Using Processing

Programming Media Art Using Processing

A Beginner's Guide

Margaret Noble

CRC Press
Taylor & Francis Group
Boca Raton London New York

CRC Press is an imprint of the
Taylor & Francis Group, an **informa** business
A CHAPMAN & HALL BOOK

First Edition published 2021
by CRC Press
6000 Broken Sound Parkway NW, Suite 300, Boca Raton, FL 33487-2742

and by CRC Press
2 Park Square, Milton Park, Abingdon, Oxon, OX14 4RN

© 2021 Margaret Noble

CRC Press is an imprint of Taylor & Francis Group, LLC

The right of Margaret Noble to be identified as author of this work has been asserted by her in accordance with sections 77 and 78 of the Copyright, Designs and Patents Act 1988.

Library of Congress Cataloging-in-Publication Data

Library of Congress Cataloging-in-Publication Data
Names: Noble, Margaret (Performance artist), author.
Title: Programming media art using processing : a beginner's guide / Margaret Noble.
Description: First edition. | Boca Raton : CRC Press, 2021. | Includes bibliographical references and index.
Identifiers: LCCN 2020038700 | ISBN 9780367508289 (paperback) | ISBN 9780367509590 (hardback) | ISBN 9781003051985 (ebook)
Subjects: LCSH: Processing (Computer program language) | Computer graphics–Computer programs. | New media art.
Classification: LCC QA76.73.P75 N63 2021 | DDC 006.6/8–dc23
LC record available at https://lccn.loc.gov/2020038700

ISBN: 978-0-367-50959-0 (hbk)
ISBN: 978-0-367-50828-9 (pbk)
ISBN: 978-1-003-05198-5 (ebk)

Typeset in Minion Pro
by KnowledgeWorks Global Ltd.

eResources for each chapter are available at www.routledge.com/9780367508289.

Contents

Acknowledgements

If it wasn't for the support I received from the community members of High Tech High, this book would not have happened. I would like to start with a very special thanks to the school leader who hired me, Robert Kuhl. Furthermore, I am grateful to the school founders: Larry Rosenstock, Rob Riordan, and Ben Daley. Their support and encouragement for over a decade of teaching (including a one-year fellowship to study computer programming) opened the door for my students and me to explore an exciting new learning environment with endless creative possibilities. I also want to recognize my collaborative colleagues throughout the years, who pushed my thinking and showed me new ways to serve my students' learning and growth.

Truth be told, I am most grateful for the collaborative learning I experienced with my students. Without the frequent input and creative production put forth by my students, I wouldn't have had the insights I needed to shape this curriculum. Every year, students revised how the class tackled challenging problems, discovered and shared new coding techniques with each other, and produced dynamic project examples for future students to build on.

These acknowledgements wouldn't be complete without a celebration of the Processing community. Thank you to Casey Reas and Ben Fry for creating such an accessible and artistic entry point into computer programming. Their Processing project has opened the door for many students who would not have previously entered it. Thank you to the Processing Foundation, which is made up of community driven educators and leaders like Daniel Shiffman. These teachers and organizers support and further these transformative learning experiences, which are highly engaging and open to all. Also, a big thank you to every kind stranger on the Processing forum who answered the many questions posted by me and my students.

Finally, thank you to my husband and my mom. They keep me believing in myself and exploring new frontiers.

Contributors

STUDENT CONTRIBUTORS

Amelia Berry

Claire Bridges

Blake Brownyard

Lorena Bustillos

JJ Chasavah

Maiah Cooper

Natalie Cote

Elijah Devillanueva

Sierra Gillingham

Flavia Huerta

Sarah Hughes

Samuel Kahn

Noah Lau

Ricardo Lednick

David Lopez

Olivia Madarang

Maelee McCarron

Tuesday Motch

Darryl Nagal

Liam Nolan

Nalani Patterson

Gillian Probert

Connor Port

Angelica Quevedo

Jakob Rosen

Tung Tran

Cianan Veltz

Kathryn Wylie

Michel Yanez

About the Author

Margaret Noble was born in Texas, raised in San Diego, and received her key artistic training in Chicago. She holds a BA in Philosophy from the University of California, San Diego, and an MFA in Studio and Sound Art from the School of the Art Institute of Chicago, Illinois.

Margaret Noble is an accomplished media producer with a background in public education, artistic production, and large-scale exhibition development. Her artworks have been exhibited nationally and internationally. Margaret Noble came to education from industry as a professional artist. Throughout her 13+ years of teaching in secondary and higher education, she has consistently supported diverse learners in producing meaningful, community-driven, multimedia projects.

Margaret and her students have also received several awards and recognitions for their classroom projects, including features in Edutopia and Wired magazine. To learn more about Margaret Noble's work, please visit: https://nobleeducator.com.

Introduction

This book is designed for learners with little or no computer programming experience and an interest in making interactive graphics. There are a variety of ways to learn computer programming and the lessons from this book were shaped by the feedback received from hundreds of students. Many of these students were intimidated by computers, while others had prior experiences with programming lessons that were frustrating or felt inaccessible. All learners are different. However, two consistent challenges were frequently expressed: (1) the illegibility of code training manuals (often due to a sea of small, black and white text) and (2) the assumption of pre-existing knowledge (even in beginning manuals). To address these concerns, this book employs a variety of strategies. The designers of Processing wrote a programming language that uses color markers to make key information visible, and this book is also published in color to clearly illustrate examples and concepts. The code examples published in this book also feature a line-by-line numbering system to help learners keep track of where they are when working through a lengthy code transcription. Furthermore, the lessons in this book are rhythmically broken down into digestible parts with code annotations and diagrams to help learners focus on the details, one step at a time. There is no assumption of any pre-existing programming experience for users of these lessons.

This book doesn't contain lectures on the history of computer programming; instead, the text is grounded in the idea of *learning by doing*. By following the lessons and producing the projects sequentially in this book, readers will develop the beginning foundational skills needed to understand computer programming basics across many languages. The first chapter introduces a series of graphical code commands, which will result in the programming of a geometric art project. With each following chapter, the programming challenges and project outcomes presented will elevate in complexity and creative opportunity. Essentially, the chapters and projects in this book provide a series of architectural structures and it is the learners who will determine what inspires them most to produce. By designing and building projects of interest, the intention is to create a learning experience that naturally flows rather than feeling like a chore or a checkbox.

A few comments and suggestions before beginning:

- Not all of the printed illustrations shown in this book are to the scale of the programmed examples.

- Once installed, the Processing interface on your computer may look slightly different from the ones pictured in this book. Not to worry – it should still work the same.

- Sometimes computers and applications glitch or crash. If this happens to you, first try quitting the Processing program and then reopen it to see if the problem goes away. If it doesn't, then try rebooting your computer. It is surprising how often these two simple steps fix tech issues.

- Sometimes, you will be frustrated with an exercise or project. That's okay – it is part of the process of problem solving. Take a break. Afterwards, approach the code problem from different angles by isolating different parts of the code and running tests.

- Sometimes it is just a typo. One misspelled word or missing semicolon can break a well-written program. Keep an eye out for the little things.

- It is strongly encouraged that you download the exercise answers and project examples from the publisher's website (www.routledge. com/9780367508289) to help you work backwards through some of the challenges you might encounter. There is no shame in starting with the answer and moving backwards to understand things more clearly.

- You may see the option to create multiple tabs within one program when coding in Processing. To keep your work consistent with the exercises and examples in this book, write your programs exclusively in one Processing tab.

- Save your work. In a world of autosaving cloud-based applications, it is easy to forget to save. However, Processing does not have an auto-save function (as of yet) and there is nothing more frustrating than losing one's hard-won work.

- It is strongly encouraged that you make sure you understand a section before moving forward to the next one since each exercise and project is designed to build on one another.

- There is always more you can explore and there are often several different ways to solve the same problem. It is advisable that you run your own supplemental experiments on the code examples provided. By doing this, you will learn a ton about how things work.

- When you experiment, save multiple versions of the same program. Sometimes a pursuit may take you down a rabbit hole and cause you to forget where you were before you started testing new ideas. To avoid this, keep a copy of your first solution attempts off to the side while you run new tests on a second version.

- Make a personal library of key code examples. It is really helpful to have a reference of favorite/useful techniques since most folks don't memorize code.

Ultimately, this is a hands-on, practical guide. The goal is to learn by doing, so let's go.

eResources for each chapter are available at www.routledge.com/ 9780367508289.

CHAPTER 1

Designing Graphically with the Language of Code

GETTING STARTED & BASIC OVERVIEW

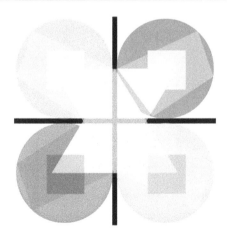

FIGURE 1.1 Student project example: geometric graphic design. (Printed with permission from Michel Yanez.)

Install Processing for free on your computer; it works on Macs, PCs, and Linux.

Link: https://processing.org/download/

FIGURE 1.2

Once on the Processing web page, scroll down to the list of "stable releases" and try to install the most recent version of Processing on your computer. If you have difficulty installing this version, then try one of the earlier releases. The projects in this book will work fine across the various versions of Processing. Once installed, open Processing and press the play button. You should see something like this.

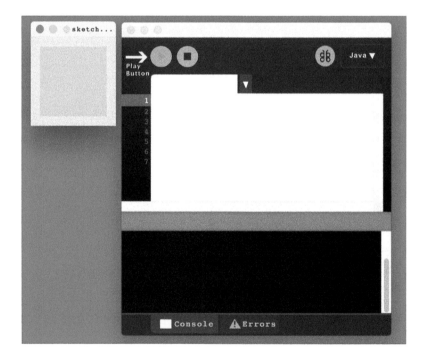

FIGURE 1.3

As shown in Figure 1.3, your Processing workspace has two windows. You enter text commands into the editor window and see your graphic results on the canvas window (also called the sketch window). You push the play button to test for results whenever you change the code.

As you move through these tutorials, it is advised that you save all of your exercises and example files for future reference.

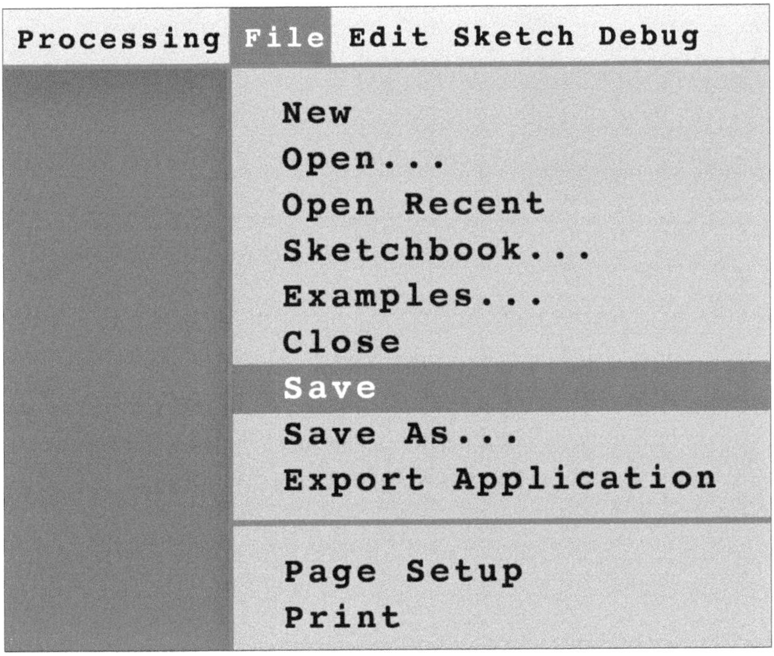

```
Processing  File  Edit  Sketch  Debug

              New
              Open...
              Open Recent
              Sketchbook...
              Examples...
              Close
              Save
              Save As...
              Export Application

              Page Setup
              Print
```

FIGURE 1.4

When you save a Processing file, you will notice that Processing automatically places a .pde file inside of a folder.

 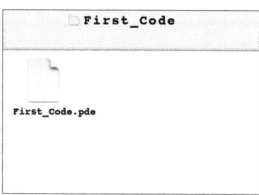

FIGURE 1.5

It is important that you keep this folder with the .pde file inside of it. Processing also requires that the folder and .pde file have the same name. When you have mismatched names between a file and a folder or separate this file path, you will get errors when opening your project.

LESSON 1.1: PIXEL GRID SYSTEM

Processing uses a pixel grid system for plotting shapes on the canvas window. Every point on the screen is a pixel and each point is specified by the locations of x, y (horizontal and vertical placements).

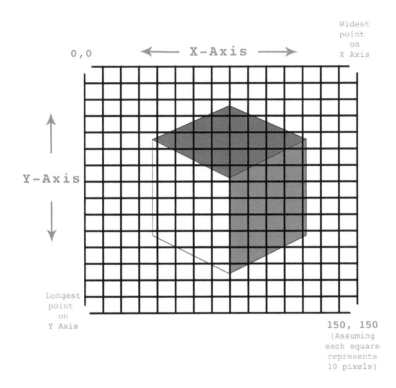

FIGURE 1.6   The longest point on the canvas is also called the height of the canvas.

The pixel grid system has its 0,0 coordinate in the *upper left corner* (this is different from beginning Algebra). The x-axis moves from left to right (0 to the specified width of your canvas). The y-axis moves from the top to the bottom, (0 to the specified height of your canvas.) This can be confusing because the "highest" point of your canvas is at the bottom of your grid.

Exercise 1.1

Grab a piece of paper and draw a quick sketch of a Processing canvas that is 100 × 100 pixels. Label the following coordinates on your paper sketch:

TABLE 1.1   Coordinates for Exercise 1.1

X	Y
0	0
100	100
50	50
0	100
100	0

LESSON 1.2: CODE AND CANVAS WINDOWS

By default, Processing opens the canvas window in the size of 100 pixels by 100 pixels. You can specify your preferred canvas dimensions by typing the command **size()** into the editor window and specifying how many pixels you want for its width and height inside of the parentheses.

```
1   size (400,200);
```

FIGURE 1.7

Important: Details matter! If the line of code you are typing uses punctuations such as parentheses, commas, brackets, and/or semicolons, then copy these details exactly.

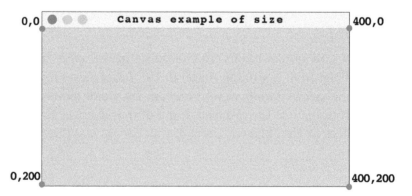

FIGURE 1.8   (Canvas size is 400 × 200).

You must also specify the background color of your canvas or it will default to gray. For now, we will use 255, which is white. More on color options soon.

```
1  size (400,200);
2  background (255);
```

FIGURE 1.9

LESSON 1.3: LINES, WIDTH, AND HEIGHT

Try this code:

```
1  size (200,100);
2  background (255);
3  line (0,0,200,100);
```

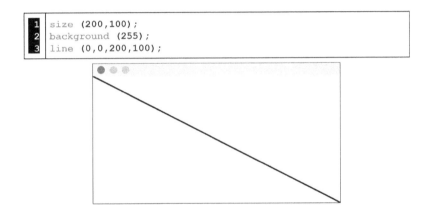

FIGURE 1.10

The words in blue are called functions (or commands). After the blue functions, the numbers inside of the parentheses are called arguments. "Arguments" are the parameters of a function(). Arguments specify the details Processing needs to draw shapes and colors in the canvas window.

```
                    Functions      Arguments
1  size (200,100);
2  background (255);
3  line (0,0,200,100);
```

FIGURE 1.11

This is how a line works…

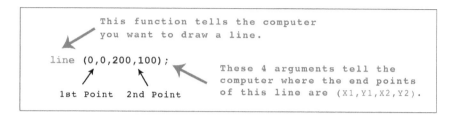

FIGURE 1.12

Try the following code to make a different **line()**. Take note of how the arguments describe each end point of the **line()**.

```
1  size (200,100);
2  background (255);
3  line (100,0,100,100);
```

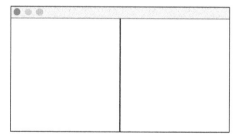

FIGURE 1.13

Try another:

```
1  size (200,100);
2  background (255);
3  line (0,50,200,50);
```

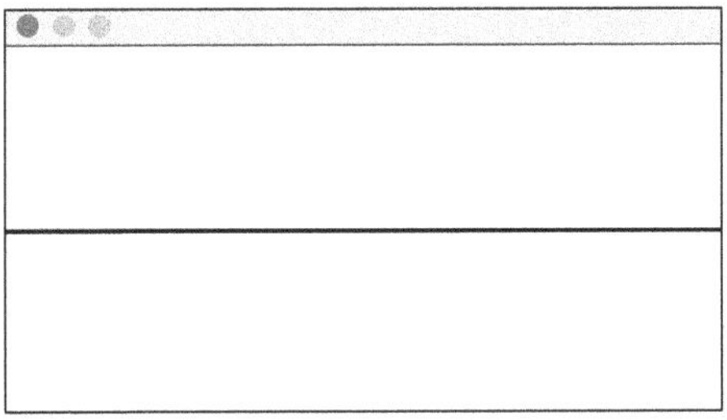

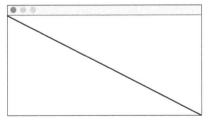

FIGURE 1.14

Make this line:

```
1  size (200,100);
2  background (255);
3  line (0,0,200,100);
```

FIGURE 1.15

Now replace the line's third and fourth arguments the words, "width" and "height" – like this:

```
1  size (200,100);
2  background (255);
3  line (0,0,width,height);
```

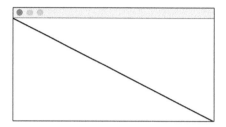

FIGURE 1.16

As you can see, the code in Figures 1.15 and 1.16 give you the same results. What do you think **width** and **height** refer to? In Processing, **width** and **height** refer back to the **size()** of the canvas. They are said to be "built-in variables" and they fluctuate in value depending on the canvas size.

```
1  size (200,100);
2  background (255);
3  line (0,0,width,height);
```

FIGURE 1.17   (In this case, **width** = 200, **height** = 100).

```
1  size (125,150);
2  background (255);
3  line (0,height,width,0);
```

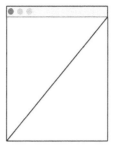

FIGURE 1.18   (In this case, **width** = 125, **height** = 150).

You can also manipulate the values of **width** and **height** with math operations.

```
1  size (200,100);
2  background (255);
3  line (width/2,50,200,height);
```

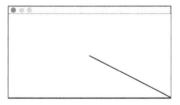

FIGURE 1.19   (**Width** = 100 (200 divided by 2) and **height** = 100).

And so on…

```
1  size (200,100);
2  background (255);
3  line (width/3,10,width/2,height);
```

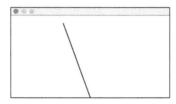

FIGURE 1.20   (**Width** = 66 (200 divided by 3, rounded up) and **height** = 100).

TABLE 1.2   Math Symbols Used in Processing

Application	Symbol
division	/
multiplication	*
addition	+
subtraction	-

There are many possible mathematical applications for designing visual art in code and **width** and **height** are very handy for thinking out graphical layouts. You can use **width** and **height** in the same program as many times as you like and in almost any numerical argument.

Exercise 1.2

Code the following picture with a 300 × 300 pixel canvas size using the built-in variables **width** and **height** in some of the **line()** arguments. It might be easiest to first code the lines with numerical arguments and then replace these values with **width** and **height** where appropriate.

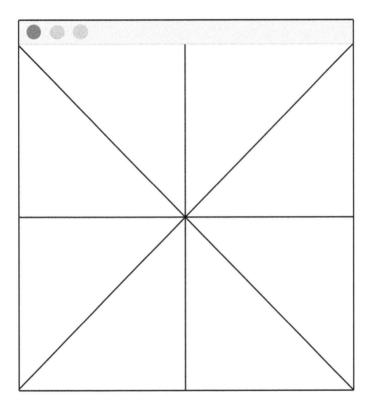

FIGURE 1.21

LESSON 1.4: MORE SHAPES

It is time to add to our graphic design tool kit as there are many shape functions we can use. Like the **line()** function, the arguments of other shape functions control different parameters. See if you can guess what the arguments control for the following shapes?

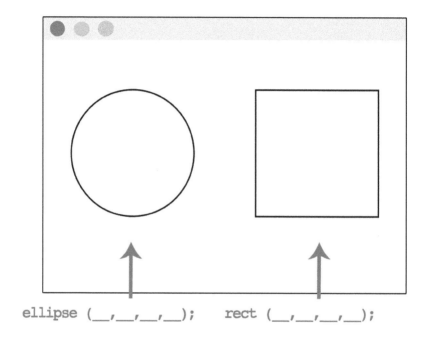

FIGURE 1.22

Answers:

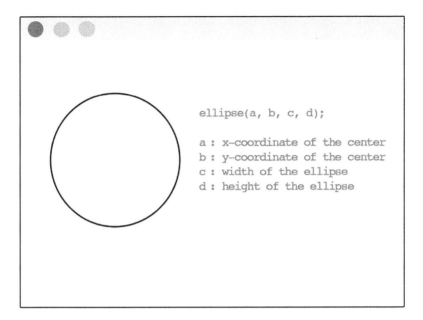

```
ellipse(a, b, c, d);

a : x-coordinate of the center
b : y-coordinate of the center
c : width of the ellipse
d : height of the ellipse
```

FIGURE 1.23

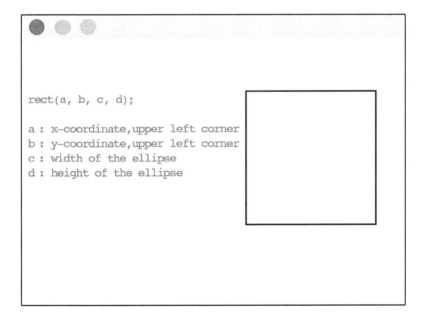

```
rect(a, b, c, d);

a : x-coordinate,upper left corner
b : y-coordinate,upper left corner
c : width of the ellipse
d : height of the ellipse
```

FIGURE 1.24

Play around with the following code to verify your understanding:

```
1  size (300,200);
2  background (255);
3  ellipse (75,100,100,100);
4  rect (175,50,100,100);
```

FIGURE 1.25

Tip: It is sometimes confusing that the x,y anchor points for the **rect()** are positioned in the upper left corner rather than in the center like the **ellipse()**. If you prefer to have your rectangle anchor points in the center, then you can add the following command before your rectangles:

rectMode (CENTER);

Exercise 1.3

Code the following two ellipses, two lines, and one rectangle on a 300 × 200 pixel sized canvas.

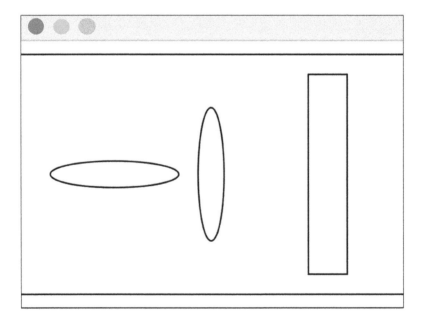

FIGURE 1.26

LESSON 1.5: GRAYSCALE

In Processing, by default lines and outlines are black, while shapes are filled white. But you can designate between grayscale tones very simply by specifying an argument of 0 (the darkest black) all the way up to 255 (the lightest white).

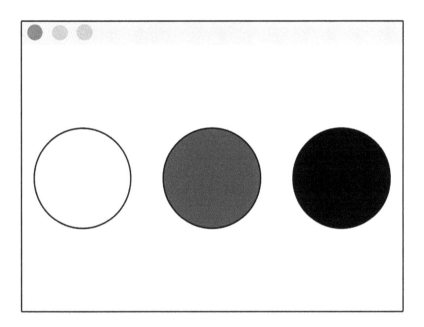

FIGURE 1.27

TABLE 1.3   Black and White Controls in Processing

In Processing	Description
fill()	Fills in the color of shapes.
stroke()	Colors the outlines of shapes and lines.
background()	Colors the background of the canvas.
0 - 255	Grayscale numerical range. 0 is black, 255 is white and all shades of gray are in between.

Exercise 1.4

Use the following starter code and complete the design pictured.

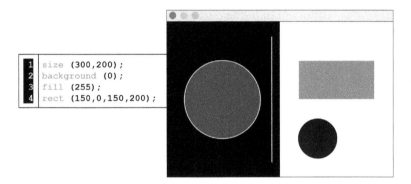

```
1  size (300,200);
2  background (0);
3  fill (255);
4  rect (150,0,150,200);
```

FIGURE 1.28

LESSON 1.6: SYNTAX, COMMENTS, AND ORDER OF CODE

Syntax

When you program the computer, you need to speak in a language that Processing understands. The syntax of a computer language is the set of rules that define the proper order and combinations of letters, numbers, and symbols. The syntax rules must be strictly followed or the computer won't be able to process your code. If you misspell words, miss punctuation, or misuse capitalizations, then your program will have errors.

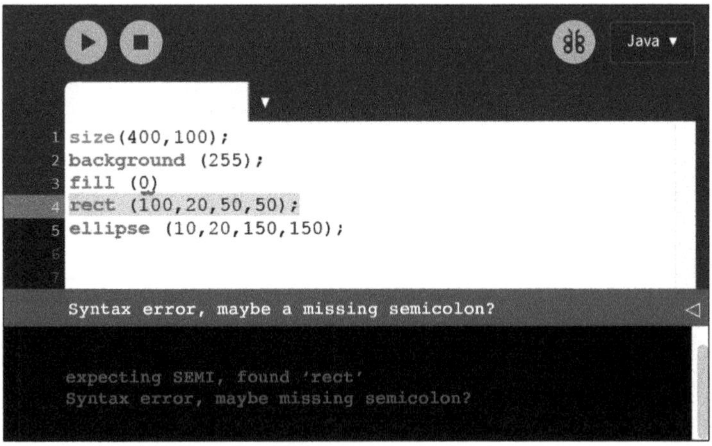

```
1  size(400,100);
2  background (255);
3  fill (0)
4  rect (100,20,50,50);
5  ellipse (10,20,150,150);
6
7

Syntax error, maybe a missing semicolon?

expecting SEMI, found 'rect'
Syntax error, maybe missing semicolon?
```

FIGURE 1.29

Processing gives you feedback on broken code in a message area below the editor. Usually, the highlighted line of code is not the problematic line. The malfunctioning line of code is often *before* the highlighted line. In Figure 1.29, the **fill**(0) is missing a semicolon.

Comments

Comments are annotations in the code to help you stay organized in a sea of text. We use two forward slashes//to indicate a comment. The two forward slashes can also be used to turn off a line of code. This is really helpful when you need to troubleshoot a problem with your program.

By isolating different lines of code, it is easier to pinpoint where issues might be.

Forward slashes used to create comments:

```
1 size (400,100);    // size of canvas
2 background (255); // sets background to white
3 stroke (0);       // sets outline color to black
4 fill (150);       // sets color shape fill to gray
```

FIGURE 1.30

Forward slashes to turn off individual lines of code commands. In Figure 1.31 below, **stroke**() and **fill**() are not read by the computer.

```
1 size (400,100);
2 background (255);
3 //stroke (0);
4 //fill (150);
```

FIGURE 1.31

There is a shorthand for turning off large chunks of code. Using /* at the beginning of the section and */ after the last line you want to turn off will render everything in between as unreadable by Processing.

```
1   /*
2   size (400,100);
3   background (255);
4   fill (0);
5   rect (100,20,50,50);
6   ellipse (10,20,150,150);
7   line (0,0, width, height);
8   rect (10,20,150,60);
9   ellipse (30,25,10,15);
10  line (0,0,width/2, height/2);
11  */
```

FIGURE 1.32

Order of Code

The order of code commands impacts how the code will run. Code lines that start at the top will impact the lines of code that come after. On the left, you see that the first gray **fill()** command is overridden by a second black **fill()** command coloring both shapes black. On the right, you see that you need to specify a new color fill before the shapes you want to be in a different color.

```
1   size (200,100);
2   background (255);
3   rectMode ( CENTER );
4   fill (100);
5   fill (0);
6   rect (50,50,50,50);
7   ellipse (150,50,50,50);
```

```
1   size (200,100);
2   background (255);
3   rectMode ( CENTER );
4   fill (0);
5   rect (50,50,50,50);
6   fill (100);
7   ellipse (150,50,50,50);
```

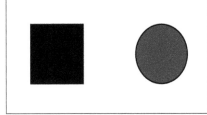

FIGURE 1.33

Exercise 1.5

Code the following on a 300 × 300 canvas.

FIGURE 1.34

LESSON 1.7: LINE COMMANDS (STROKE AND NO STROKE)

In your designs, you may want to manipulate the look of lines and outlines. Here are two new commands for modifying lines in your projects.

TABLE 1.4   Line Commands

Command	Description
noStroke()	Removes outlines on shapes.
strokeWeight()	Changes the thickness of lines and shape outlines.

Exercise 1.6

Code the following image on a 200 × 200 pixel canvas and annotate your code with organizational comments.

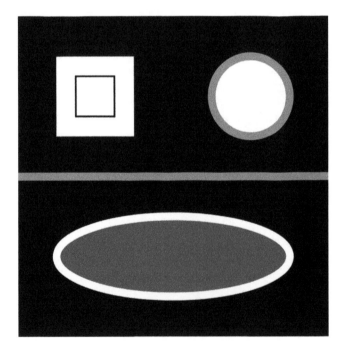

FIGURE 1.35

LESSON 1.8: COLORING PIXELS

In the art class, the primary colors were red, yellow, and blue. In the digital environment, our primary colors are red, green, and blue also known as RGB. These are the colors of light.

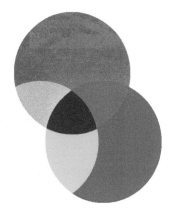 

Primary analogue color mixing.   **RGB digital color mixing.**

FIGURE 1.36

TABLE 1.5   Processing Color Use Overview

Description	Examples	
Color functions commonly used:	**fill**()	//colors the inside of shapes
	stroke()	//colors lines and outlines
Code functions using R,G,B color have 3 arguments. One argument for each color (red, green, and blue).	**fill** (255, 0, 0) ;	// red
	stroke (0, 255, 0) ;	// green
	fill (0, 0, 255) ;	// blue
Code functions using grayscale color have 1 argument.	**stroke** (0);	// black
	fill (255):	// white
RGB color values range from 0 to 255. 0 is the darkest and 255 is the lightest.	**stroke** (0, 25, 0);	//dark green
	fill (0, 0, 255);	// bright blue
Colors that are not primary red, green, and blue are made by various mixes of these 3.	**fill** (150, 0,100);	//dark wine color
	stroke (173, 201, 20);	// lime green color

Play with this code to see R, G, B (red, green, blue) arguments in action.

```
1  size (400,200);
2  background (255,0,0);
3  rectMode ( CENTER );
4  fill (0,0,255);
5  rect (200,100,200,80);
6  stroke (255,255,0);
7  strokeWeight (10);
8  fill (0,255,0);
9  ellipse (200,100,300,25);
10 stroke (255);
11 line (0,0,400,200);
12 stroke (0);
13 line (400,0,0,200);
```

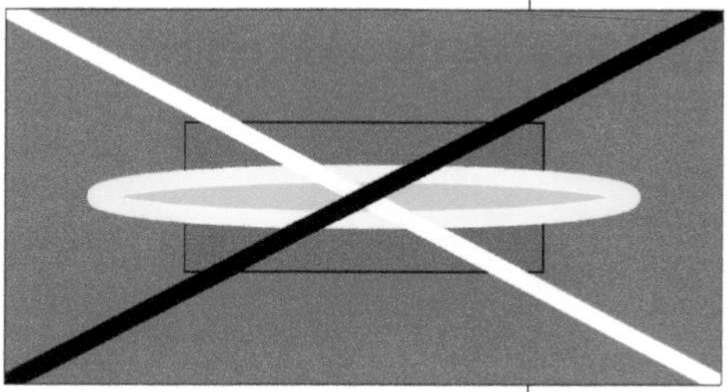

FIGURE 1.37

Tip: Processing has a color selector that gives you the exact RGB mix for a specified color.

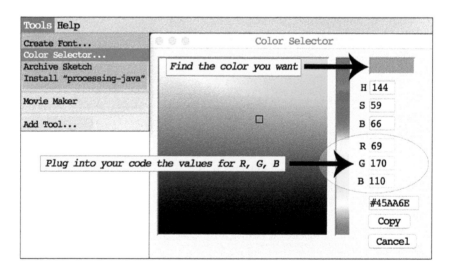

FIGURE 1.38

Exercise 1.7

Code the following sketch on a 300 × 300 canvas.

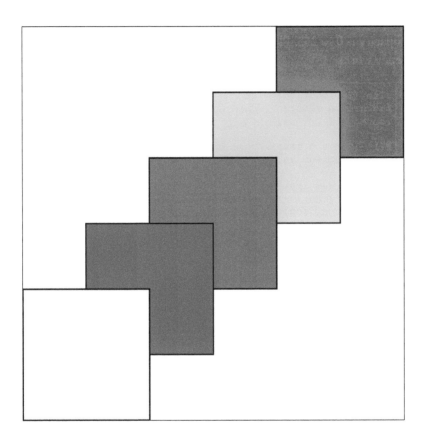

FIGURE 1.39

LESSON 1.9: ADDING TRANSPARENCY VALUES

Some really nice results can be achieved by adding transparency to your designs. For color, add a fourth argument to your R,G,B formulation to specify opacity. For grayscale, add a second argument. The number range for opacity is 0 to 255. Play with the following program to see how transparency works.

```
1  size (200,100);
2  background (255); //solid white background
3  rectMode (CENTER);
4
5  fill (255,0,0,100); //red shape fill w/transparency
6  rect (100, 50, 75, 75);
7
8  strokeWeight (20);
9  stroke (0, 50); //black line/outline stroke w/transparency
10 line (100,0, 100, height);
11
12 fill (0,0,255,175); //blue shape fill w/transparency
13 ellipse (100,50,190,20);
14
15 noStroke ();
16 fill (0,255,0); //green shape fill no transparency
17 ellipse (100,50,25,25);
```

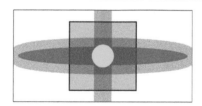

FIGURE 1.40

Exercise 1.8

Type the following starter code:

```
1  size (400,250);
2  background (255);
3  fill (0,0,255,150);
4  ellipse (50,50,100,100);
5  fill (255,0,0,150);
6  ellipse (100,100,100,100);
```

FIGURE 1.41

Next, add four more circles to match the following design:

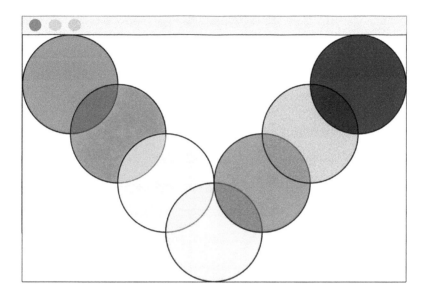

FIGURE 1.42

LESSON 1.10: THE PROCESSING REFERENCE – IMPORTANT RESOURCE!

The reference is a comprehensive, online library of code commands available for use in Processing. It is an important place to figure out things not covered in this book and will also expand your knowledge of things you already know. For the purposes of this chapter, we are going to use the reference to learn about more 2D shapes.

Go to https://processing.org/reference/ to find the following page.

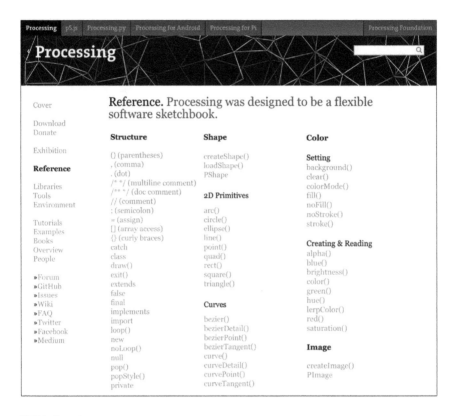

FIGURE 1.43

First, navigate to the "2D Primitives" category. Here you will find many more possible shapes available for your projects. Next, click on the **quad()** function to open its dedicated page. The following diagram uses the **quad()** entry as an example on how to navigate the reference pages.

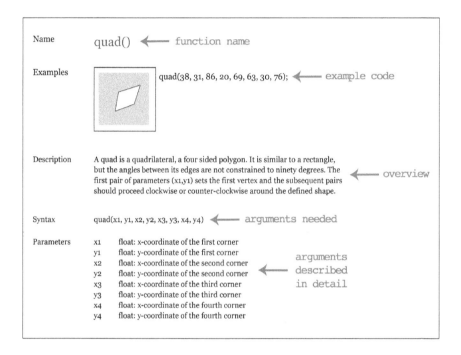

FIGURE 1.44

PROJECT: GEOMETRIC DESIGN

Code a geometrically patterned design with a variety of different shapes using the colors of your choice. Aim to go beyond lines, rects, and ellipses with new 2D shapes from the Processing reference. For project examples, see the download folder available from the publisher's website.

FIGURE 1.45 Student project example: geometric graphic design. (Printed with permission from Flavia Huerta.)

CHAPTER 2

Creating Responsive Environments

FIGURE 2.1   Student project example: interactive environment. (Printed with permission from Flavia Huerta.)

In this chapter, we will design 2D environments that are interactive! Shapes will move, grow, and color shift in response to the computer mouse.

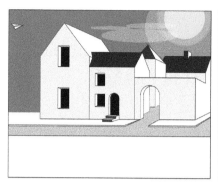

FIGURE 2.2   Student project example: interactive environment. (Printed with permission from Noah Lau.)

LESSON 2.1: DYNAMIC COMPUTER PROGRAMS

In Chapter 1, the programs we wrote were static – the shapes stayed in place at the coordinates they were plotted. In order to create shapes that animate, we need to write programs that are dynamic.

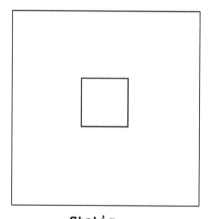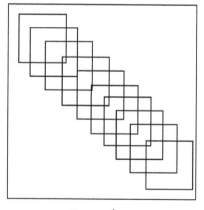

Static.   **Dynamic.**

FIGURE 2.3

These "dynamic" programs are a directional series of events comprised of graphical animations that respond to user input. We can look at the stages of an arcade video game to help us envision how we will code our active projects in Processing.

TABLE 2.1   Video Game Stages

1) Users prepare to play, the computer program *sets-up*.	2) Once the *setup* is complete, the conditions of the game are initialized and the computer *draws* animations in response to user input.

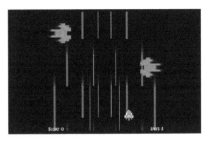

3) This cycle continues and the computer program *draws* new graphics that shift and vary with each new instruction or interaction.	4) Eventually, the cycle ends.

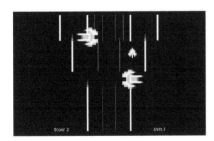

Figure 2.3 and Table 2.1 represent stills from a student Processing project (printed with permission from Blake Brownyard).

Technically, we will add two new structures to make our programs dynamic: **void setup()** and **void draw()**. These two structures function differently, **void setup()** loads code commands *once* – much like a start-up screen. With **void draw()**, the code commands run continuously, and it is this procedure that allows for animation. It is important to take note of their shared syntax styles. Processing presents **void setup()** and **void draw()** in the colors green and blue, followed by an empty parentheses set.

```
1   void setup () {
2     //code lines here
3       //code lines here
4         //code lines here
5   }
6
7   void draw () {
8     //code lines here
9       //code lines here
10        //code lines here
11  }
```

FIGURE 2.4

The curly brackets we see after the parentheses hold the code commands "inside" of **void setup()** or **void draw()**.

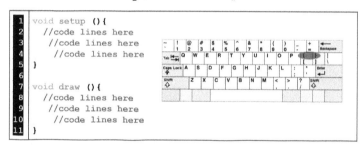

```
1   void setup () {
2     //code lines here
3       //code lines here
4         //code lines here
5   }
6
7   void draw () {
8     //code lines here
9       //code lines here
10        //code lines here
11  }
```

FIGURE 2.5

TABLE 2.2   Void Setup() and Void Draw() Overview

Summary	Notes
Code in curly brackets {}	Now that we have entered dynamic programming, from now on, all of your code lines/functions will be inside a pair of curly brackets associated with active structures like **void setup()** and **void draw()**. If some of your commands are not contained within curly brackets while other lines are, you will get errors from the Processing console that read, "you're mixing active and static modes."
void setup() runs once.	You will use **void setup()** for code commands that only need to happen once. For example, the **size()** command will go inside of **void setup()** because canvas sizes don't fluctuate.
void draw() runs continually.	**void draw()** is continually running and updating the animation frames. The majority of your dynamic animations and interactions will be programmed inside of **void draw()**.

Exercise 2.1

Think back to your geometric design project from the previous chapter. If you could animate the various shapes you used before, what would you do? Make a list of four or more simple animations you would like to implement.

LESSON 2.2: FIRST ANIMATIONS

Type and run the following code:

```
1    void setup() {
2    size (700,400);
3    }
4
5    void draw () {
6    background (0,0,250);
7
8    //sun
9    stroke (0);
10   fill (255,0,0);
11   ellipse (350,350,750,250);
12
13   //Building Structure
14   fill (0);
15   rect (500,120,200,300);
16   fill (150);
17   quad (500,120,450,200,450,420,500,420);
18
19   //Windows
20   fill (255,255,0);
21   rect (530,150,150,40);
22   rect (530,200,150,40);
23   rect (530,250,150,40);
24   rect (530,300,150,40);
25   rect (530,350,150,40);
26   }
```

FIGURE 2.6   Example design printed with permission from Ricardo Lednick.

If you run the above code and see the same picture, this means that you have correctly implemented a visual design within the structures of **void setup()** and **void draw()**. Now, we can have some fun and animate this design. As previously mentioned, **void draw()** is constantly updating frames. Right now, nothing is animated because the arguments inside of **void draw()** are static numbers. Remember "functions" and "arguments" from the last chapter?

```
              Functions: action commands in blue.
                        Arguments: the specific parameters of each
stroke (0);                        function, stored in parentheses().
fill (255,0,0);
ellipse (350,350,750,250);
```

FIGURE 2.7

We need argument values that change over time in order to animate our designs. Processing has two built-in variables we can use to get things moving: **mouseX** and **mouseY**. In the previous example (Figure 2.6), animate the red color **fill()** of the sun by replacing the argument 255 with **mouseX** like this:

```
8  //sun
9  stroke (0);
10 fill (mouseX,0,0);
11 ellipse (350,350,750,250);
```

FIGURE 2.8

Now, move your computer mouse from left to right to see what changes. Next, replace the height argument of the **ellipse()** with **mouseY** like this:

```
8  //sun
9  stroke (0);
10 fill (mouseX,0,0);
11 ellipse (350,350,750,mouseY);
```

FIGURE 2.9

Now, move your mouse up and down. As you can see, **mouseY** fluctuates in value depending on where the mouse moves vertically. And, **mouseX** fluctuates in value depending on where the mouse moves horizontally. It is as if the canvas window is a mouse pad. See the following diagram for understanding how **mouseX** and **mouseY** vary depending on your mouse's position.

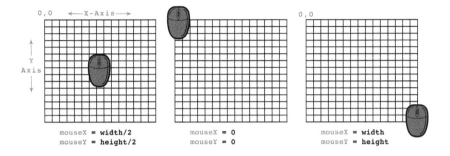

mouseX = width/2   mouseX = 0   mouseX = width
mouseY = height/2   mouseY = 0   mouseY = height

FIGURE 2.10

You can use **mouseX** and **mouseY** multiple times throughout your code in any numerical argument. Try plugging **mouseX** and **mouseY** in various places to see what animations you can create. You can use **mouseX** and **mouseY** to grow/shrink shapes, fade colors/transparencies, move shapes around, and so much more.

TABLE 2.3   Examples of MouseX and MouseY Animation Applications

Code Example	Animation
fill (0, 255, 0, **mouseY**):	The green fill will become transparent when the mouse is moved up and then return to full opacity when the mouse is moved down.
strokeWeight (**mouseX**);	The line/outline thickness of shapes that follow this command will grow and shrink when the mouse is moved left and right.
ellipse (100,100, 50, **mouseY**);	The ellipse will change size from tall to short when the mouse is moved up and down.
rect (**mouseX, mouseY**, 50, 50);	The rectangle will follow the mouse on both X and Y axes.
rect (**mouseX***.5, 50, 50, 50);	The rectangle will follow the mouse on the horizontal axis but will be limited in its range because mouseX is multiplied by .5 (thus steadily decreasing). See Table 1. 2 from Chapter 1 for math symbols used in Processing.

Exercise 2.2

Program the following starter lines of code:

```
1  void setup(){
2  size(400,400);
3  } //close setup
4
5  void draw(){
6  background(255,255,0);
7  noStroke();
8  fill (255,0,255);
9  ellipse (100, 100, 200, 200);
10 fill (0, 255, 255);
11 rectMode (CENTER);
12 rect (300,200,100, 350);
13 strokeWeight (10);
14 stroke (0,0,255);
15 line (0, height/2, width, height/2);
16 } //close draw
```

FIGURE 2.11

a. Make the light blue **rect()** move up and down with the mouse.

b. Make the pink **ellipse()** grow evenly when the mouse is moved left and right.

c. Make the dark blue **line()** turn invisible when the mouse is moved up and down.

d. Make the **background()** cycle through multiple colors when the mouse is moved around in a circle.

LESSON 2.3: ANIMATION TRAILS

Type the following code and move your mouse around:

```
1  void setup (){
2  size (300,300);
3
4  } //closes setup
5
6  void draw() {
7
8  background (0);
9  strokeWeight (3);
10 stroke (0,255,0); //green line color
11
12 //1st point static at 0,0 and 2nd point follows mouse
13 line (0,0,mouseX,mouseY);
14
15 stroke (255,0,0); //red line color
16
17 //1st point follows mouse and 2nd point static at 300,300
18 line (mouseX,mouseY,300,300);
19
20 } //closes draw
21
22
23
24
25
26
27
```

FIGURE 2.12

As discussed earlier, **void setup()** and **void draw()** operate differently. To see this difference in action, move the **background()** command from **void draw()** into **void setup().**

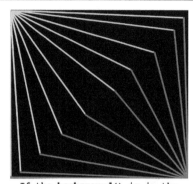

If the **background()** is in the **setup()** then it will update only once. Consequently, every animation movement in draw() will be visible.	If the **background()** is in **draw()** then it will continually update. Every animation movement will be covered by the background each time draw() cycles through.

FIGURE 2.13

In most complex designs, you will usually want your **background()** in **void draw()** to avoid unwanted animation artifacts. But, for simpler line/ shape animations these trails are fun.

Exercise 2.3

Create your own unique animation design with shape trails.

LESSON 2.4: FINDING EXACT COORDINATES

Maybe you are tired of guessing where the exact x,y coordinates are when drawing a shape in a specific place? We have two new tools to help with this issue: **println()** and **void mousePressed()**.

Type and run the following code. Click your mouse where the black lines intersect.

```
1  void setup() {
2  size(300, 100);
3  } //close setup
4
5  void draw() {
6  background(255);
7  strokeWeight (10);
8  stroke (0); //black lines
9  line (50,0,50,100);
10 line (100,0,100,100);
11 line (150,0,150,100);
12 line (200,0,200,100);
13 line (250,0,250,100);
14 line (0,50,300,50);
15 stroke (255,0,0); //red outline
16 fill (0,0);
17 ellipse (mouseX,mouseY,35,35);
18 } //close draw
19
20 void mousePressed() {
21 println("mouseX=", mouseX, "mouseY=", mouseY);
22 } //closes mousePressed
```

FIGURE 2.14

If you look at the bottom of your Processing editor window to the black console, you will see values for **mouseX** and **mouseY** wherever you clicked in the canvas window.

mouseX= 4 mouseY= 52

FIGURE 2.15

It is the **println()** function that writes information to the black console area. In Figure 2.14, we configured **println()** to report on the position of **mouseX** and **mouseY** inside of the active structure **mousePressed()**. This strategy is really helpful for precise control over graphic design. First, we will look at the syntax used with the **println()** function:

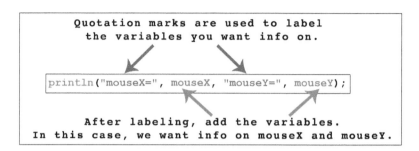

FIGURE 2.16

The other new structure shown in Figure 2.14 is **void mousePressed()**. The **void mousePressed()** structure functions as its own self-contained entity using curly brackets just like **void setup()** and **void draw()**.

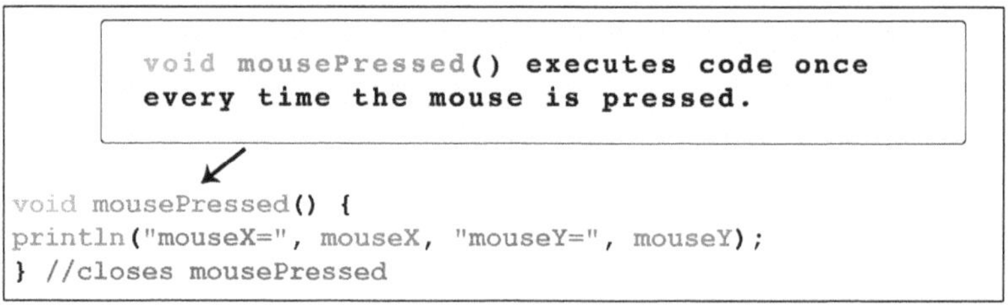

```
void mousePressed() executes code once
every time the mouse is pressed.

void mousePressed() {
println("mouseX=", mouseX, "mouseY=", mouseY);
} //closes mousePressed
```

FIGURE 2.17

Exercise 2.4

FIGURE 2.18

a. Use the **println()** function with **void mousePressed()** to insert a blue triangle, as shown above (see code from Figure 2.14). If you haven't learned how to make a triangle yet, look it up on the Processing website reference: https://processing.org/reference/ under 2D Primitives.

b. Move the red outlined **ellipse()** from **void draw()** to **void mousePressed()**. Run the code and explain why this happens.

c. Now, move the **background()** from **void draw()** into **void setup()**. Run the code and explain why this happens.

LESSON 2.5: COMPLEX SHAPES

FIGURE 2.19

If you want a custom shape with multiple vertices, you can use the **begin-Shape()** command. Here's how:

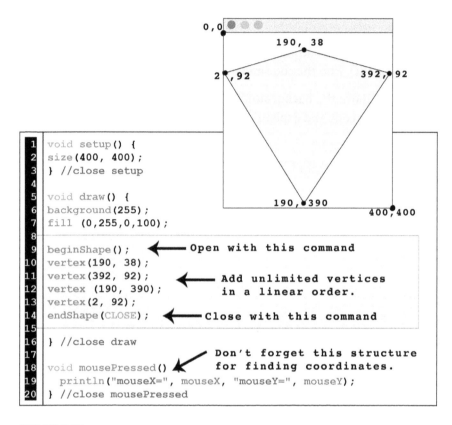

FIGURE 2.20

Exercise 2.5

Create your own multi-pointed silhouette shape using **beginShape()**.

LESSON 2.6: LINKING SHAPES FOR SYNCHED MOVEMENT

Type and play the following program:

```
1  void setup(){
2  size(400,400);
3  }
4
5  void draw(){
6  background(172,129,180);
7
8  //head
9  fill (255,255,255);
10 ellipse (mouseX,mouseY,300,200);
11
12 //eyes
13 fill (0,0,0);
14 ellipse (mouseX,mouseY,50,50);
15 ellipse (mouseX,mouseY,50,50);
16
17 //mouth
18 rectMode (CENTER);
19 fill (255,0,0);
20 rect (mouseX, mouseY,100,25);
21 }
```

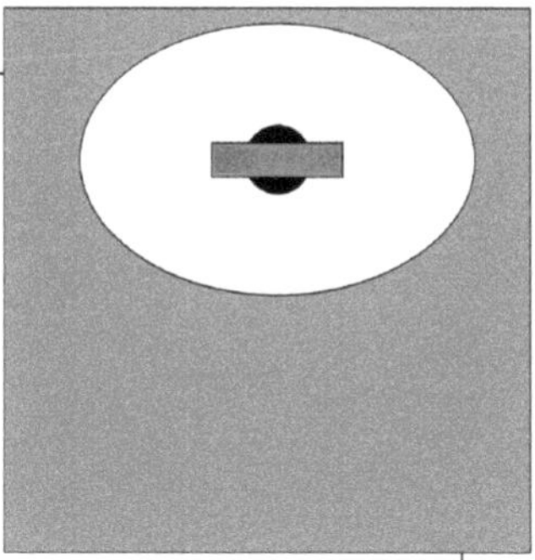

FIGURE 2.21

Although there are comments labeling "eyes", "mouth", and "head" in the code – there is no discernable face. The shapes are stacked on top of each other in relation to **mouseX** and **mouseY**. To create definition in our moving designs, we can offset the shapes with simple math.

```
1  void setup(){
2  size(400,400);
3  }
4
5  void draw(){
6  background(172,129,180);
7
8  //head
9  fill (255);
10 ellipse (mouseX,mouseY,300,200);
11
12 //eyes
13 fill (0);
14 ellipse (mouseX-100,mouseY,50,50);  //offset left eye -100
15 ellipse (mouseX+100,mouseY,50,50);  //offset right eye +100
16
17 //mouth
18 rectMode (CENTER);
19 fill (255,0,0);
20 rect (mouseX, mouseY+50,100,25);  //offset mouth down +50
21 }
```

FIGURE 2.22

Exercise 2.6

Using the starter code from Figure 2.22, add three more design details to move with the mouse. For example: add a hat, eyebrows, ears, or other accessories of your choice.

LESSON 2.7: ADDING TEXT

You may want to add labels or instructions in your designs. Here's how text works:

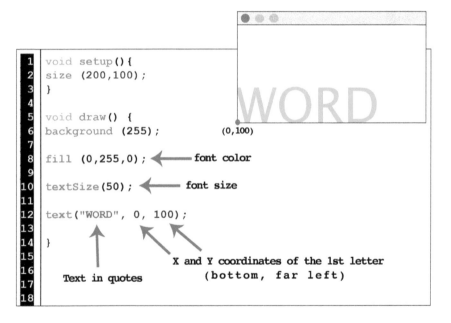

FIGURE 2.23

If you don't like the anchor position for placing text (bottom, far left), you can explore other anchor positions with the additional command, **textAlign()**. See explanation on the Processing Reference (https://processing.org/reference/).

Exercise 2.7

Code the following text design on a 200 × 100 sized canvas. Don't forget to use void **mousePressed()** with **println()** to help you find the coordinates.

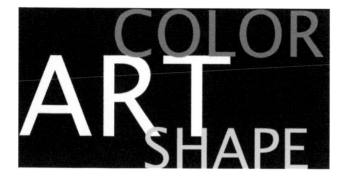

FIGURE 2.24

LESSON 2.8: ROTATING SHAPES

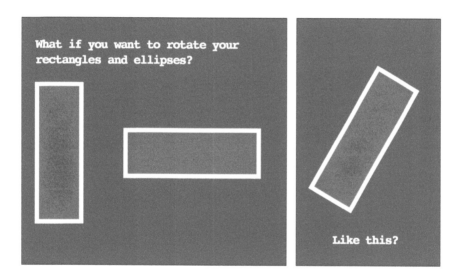

FIGURE 2.25

We will use the **rotate()** command and radian degrees to spin rectangles and ellipses into new positions. In order to do this, it is helpful to use some modifying commands in our code. Run the following program:

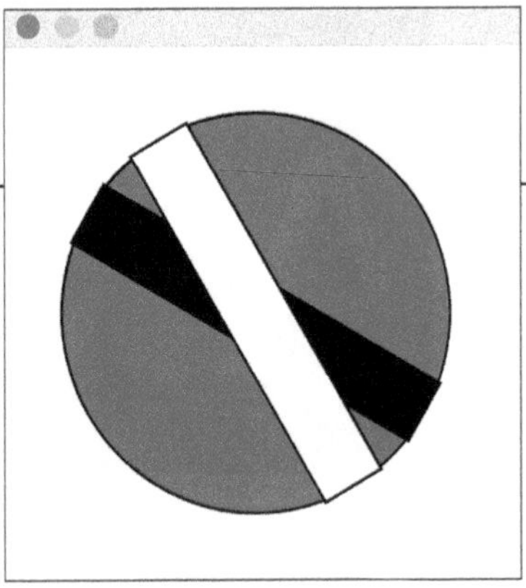

```
1  void setup (){
2  size (200,200);
3  }
4
5  void draw() {
6  background (255);
7  fill (255,0,0);
8  ellipse (100,100,150,150);
9  rectMode (CENTER);
10
11 //BLACK ROTATED RECT
12 pushMatrix (); //start temporary change to the grid system
13 translate (100,100); //move 0,0 position to 100,100
14 rotate(radians(30)); //rotate to 30 radians
15 fill (0);
16 rect (0,0,150,25);
17 popMatrix(); //end temporary change to the grid system
18
19
20 //WHITE ROTATED RECT (Same as black rect but new angle)
21 pushMatrix ();
22 translate (100,100);
23 rotate (radians(60)); //rotate to 60 radians
24 fill (255);
25 rect (0,0,150,25);
26 popMatrix();
27
28 } //close draw
```

FIGURE 2.26

TABLE 2.4   Rotate() Overview

Code Command	Explanation
pushMatrix();	Use this command to begin a temporary grid transformation.
translate (100,100);	Move the 0,0 position of the X,Y pixel grid system to the center of the shape you want to rotate.

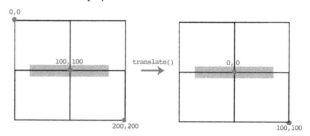

rotate (radians (30); **rotate (radians** (60);	The **rotate()** function rotates *the entire coordinate system* around the origin. In Figure 2.26, the black rectangle is at 30 radian degrees and the white rectangle is at 60 radian degrees. Here is a diagram of how *Processing* measures angles in degrees:

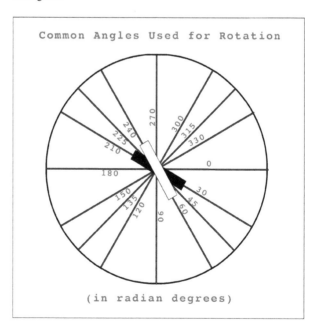

popMatrix();	Close the temporary transformation of the pixel grid system.

Exercise 2.8

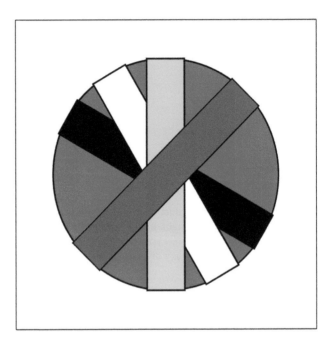

FIGURE 2.27

a. Using the previous code example (Figure 2.26), finish the pictured design above.

b. Now add **+mouseX** to each of the **radian()** values and test what animates when you move the mouse.

PROJECT: INTERACTIVE ENVIRONMENT

Make a place. It can be a landscape, spacescape, cityscape, or other specific place/environment that has transforming or moving parts which respond to the mouse. You can make things grow, move, fade, or change color. Aim to have a minimum of eight unique animated mouse interactions. See project examples in the downloads folder available from the publisher's website. Art challenge: design your place in perspective considering directional light and object angles.

FIGURE 2.28   Student project example: interactive environment. (Printed with permission from David Lopez.)

FIGURE 2.29   Student project example: interactive environment. (Printed with permission from Natalie Cote.)

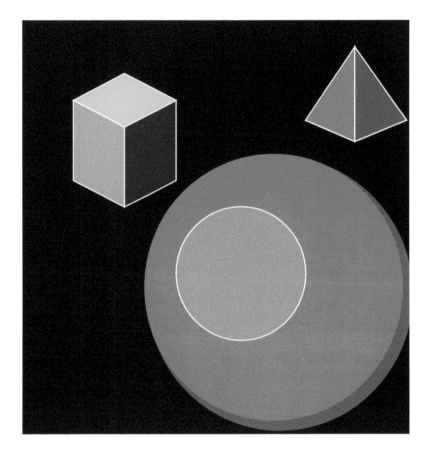

FIGURE 2.30 Design tip: each 3D object shown here is made of layered flat shapes.

CHAPTER 3

Automated Animations

FIGURE 3.1 Student project example: animated art project. (Printed with permission from Lorena Bustillos.)

In Chapter 2, we programmed interactive animations that were responsive to computer mouse movements. Now, we are going to automate our animations by writing custom variables that trigger events when the program starts. This new strategy will allow us to automatically start with visual changes in movement, shape, and color. Design details like rising moons and clock rotations will come to life, pushing our projects into more interesting domains.

FIGURE 3.2   Student project example: animated art project. (Printed with permission from Kathryn Wylie.)

LESSON 3.1: COUNTING VARIABLES

To automate our animation designs, we will use numerical variables that count up or down. We have already used two variables built into the Processing language, **mouseX** and **mouseY**. These two count up or down in sync with computer mouse movements. Now, we are going to write our own custom variables that automatically move up or down in value.

Run the following program:

```
1  int moveright = 10;
2
3  void setup() {
4  size (400,200);
5  }//close setup
6
7  void draw() {
8  background (0,255,100);
9  fill (162, 61, 252);
10 ellipse (moveright, 100, 150, 150);
11
12 moveright = moveright + 1;
13
14 }//close draw
```

FIGURE 3.3

If you see the purple circle traveling from left to right, then you have successfully written your first custom variable animation. So, what is new here?

```
1   int moveright = 10;  ⟵——— 1) We declared a variable.
2
3   void setup() {
4   size (400,200);
5   }//close setup
6
7   void draw() {
8   background (0,255,100);
9   fill (162, 61, 252);
10  ellipse (moveright, 100, 150, 150); ⟵——— 2) We placed it.
11
12  moveright = moveright + 1; ⟵
13
14  }//close draw                       3) We assigned an operation to it.
```

FIGURE 3.4

These three steps are essential for using custom variables. As with all computer programming, the syntax must be strictly adhered to. Do not ignore the placement of semicolons, equal signs or other punctuations. The following diagrams (Figures 3.5–3.7), present a detailed overview of the three steps needed to implement custom variables.

Step 1:
Declare the variable.

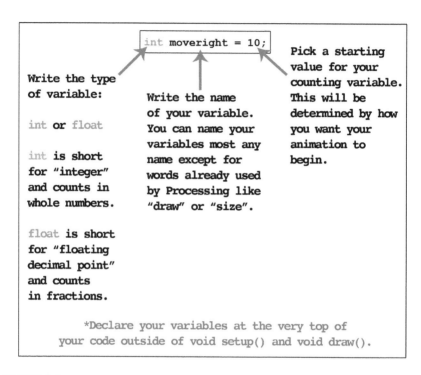

FIGURE 3.5

Step 2:
Place your variable in the argument you want to animate.

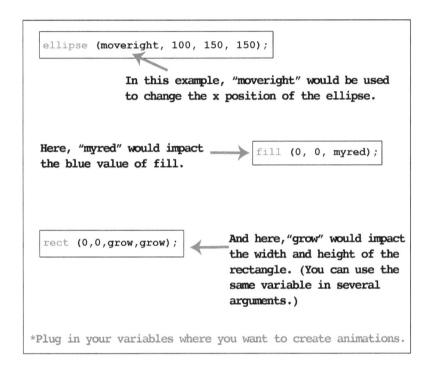

In this example, "moveright" would be used
to change the x position of the ellipse.

Here, "myred" would impact
the blue value of fill.

And here, "grow" would impact
the width and height of the
rectangle. (You can use the
same variable in several
arguments.)

*Plug in your variables where you want to create animations.

FIGURE 3.6

Step 3:

Write an assignment operator to make your variable change over time.

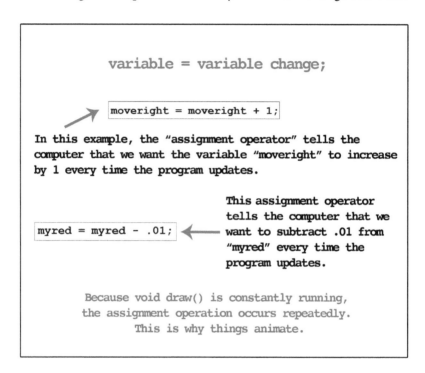

FIGURE 3.7

Now, we will put it all together but this time using a float variable. Run the following program to stretch the yellow ellipse:

```
1  float banana = 50; //declare the variable
2
3  void setup() {
4  size (400, 200);
5  }
6
7  void draw () {
8  background (0);
9
10 //banana
11 fill (213, 250, 10);
12 ellipse (200, 100, banana, 50);//place the variable
13
14 //orange
15 fill (250, 121, 15);
16 ellipse (200, 30, 50, 50);
17
18 //assignment operator
19 banana = banana + .9;//write an assignment operator
20
21 } //close draw
```

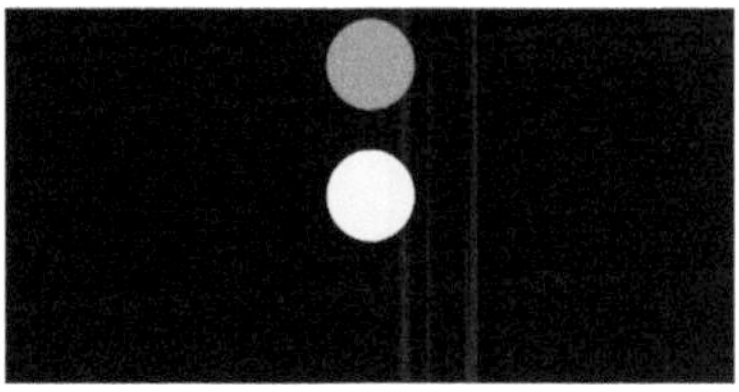

FIGURE 3.8

Exercise 3.1

a. Start with the previous code from Figure 3.8 and write a new custom variable that animates the orange ellipse to move down.

b. Write a third custom variable and animate the background to change from black to white.

LESSON 3.2 MOVING OBJECTS IN MULTIPLE DIRECTIONS

Depending on your animation goals, you may want to have variables start off-screen or move backwards. Below is a diagram explaining how these two work:

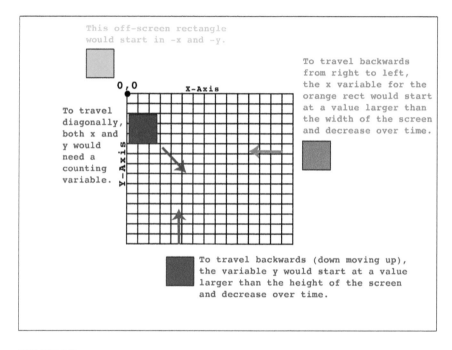

FIGURE 3.9

Exercise 3.2

Run the following starter code:

```
1  void setup() {
2  size (200, 200);
3  }
4
5  void draw () {
6  background (255);
7  rectMode (CENTER);
8
9  //left yellow rect
10 fill (213, 250, 10);
11 rect (30, 100, 50, 50);
12
13 //right orange rect
14 fill (250, 121, 15);
15 rect (170, 100, 50, 50);
16
17 //top green rect
18 fill (0, 121, 15);
19 rect (100, 30, 50, 50);
20
21 //bottom blue rect
22 fill (0, 21, 150);
23 rect (100, 170, 50, 50);
24
25 //right corner purple rect
26 fill (160, 58, 134);
27 rect (30, 30, 50, 50);
28 } //close draw
```

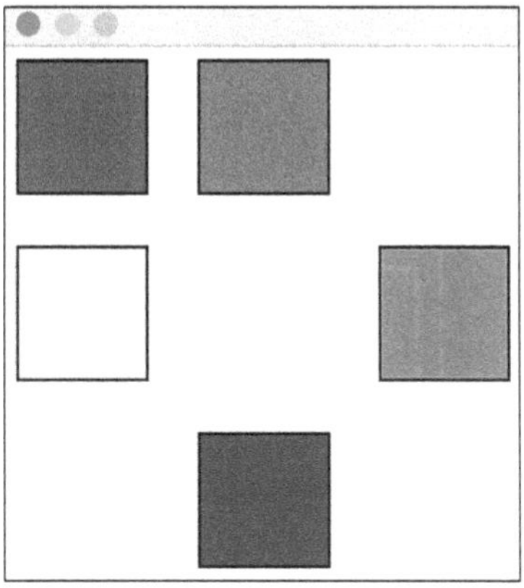

FIGURE 3.10

Now, using custom variables make each square travel in the following directions at different speeds:

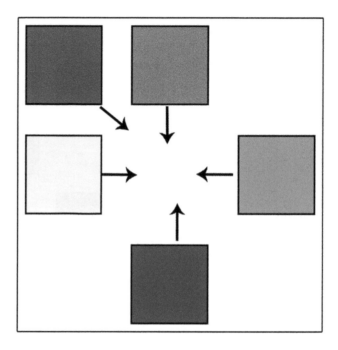

FIGURE 3.11

LESSON 3.3 GROWING SHAPES WITH THE MOUSE

In the following program, you will see three examples of custom variables making shapes grow.

Run the code:

```
1  int growcirc = 5;
2  float growmore = 25;
3  float growln = 150;
4
5  void setup (){
6  size (300,300);
7  }
8
9  void draw(){
10 background (255);
11 rectMode (CENTER);
12
13 //ellipse
14 noStroke();
15 fill (0,0,255,100);
16 ellipse (150, 150, growcirc, growcirc); //size grows even
17
18 //rect
19 fill (0);
20 rect (150, 150, 50,growmore); //grows only in the height
21
22 //line
23 stroke (255);
24 strokeWeight (5);
25 line (growln, 150, 150, 150); //stretches X1 point left
26
27 //assignment operators
28 growcirc = growcirc + 4;
29 growmore = growmore + 3;
30 growln = growln - .5;
31 } //close draw
```

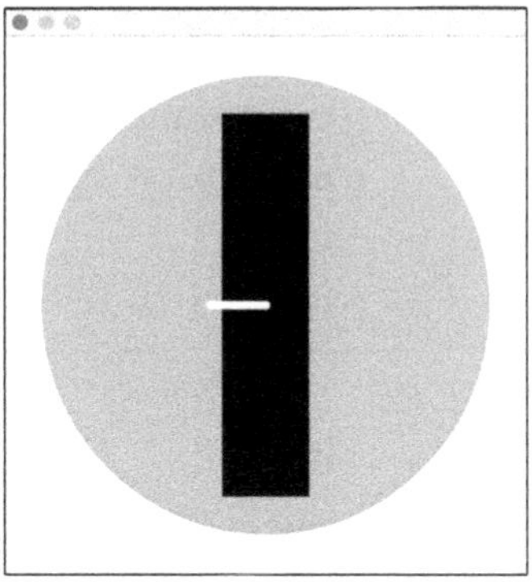

FIGURE 3.12

What if you want the shapes to animate only when you click the mouse?

Add a **void mousePressed()** to the previous example and move your assignment operators from **void draw()** to inside of it:

```
void mousePressed(){

//assignment operators
  growcirc = growcirc + 4;
  growmore = growmore + 3;
  growln = growln - .5;

}//close mousePressed
```

FIGURE 3.13

Test the code. If you press the mouse several times, your shapes should transform. To see more dramatic transformations with each click, make your assignment operator values larger.

Exercise 3.3

Add onto the previous example (Figures 3.12–3.13) the following animations:

a. Code a second black rectangle in the center of the canvas that grows in width only when the mouse is pressed.

b. Code a second white line in the center of the canvas that stretches down only when the mouse is pressed.

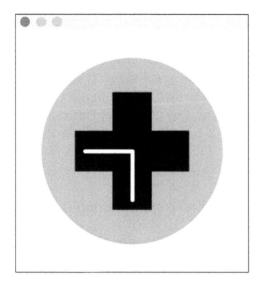

FIGURE 3.14

LESSON 3.4: PRINTLN() FOR DEBUGGING

Run the following program:

```
1  int fadein = 255;
2  float movedown = 100;
3
4  void setup() {
5  size (200,200);
6  }
7
8  void draw() {
9  background (12, 222, 240);
10
11 //red triangle fades in
12 fill (255,0,0, fadein);
13 triangle (0,200,100,0,200,200);
14
15 //white ellipse moves down
16 fill (255);
17 ellipse (100, movedown, 50, 50);
18
19 //assignment operators
20 fadein = fadein + 1;
21 movedown = movedown + .001;
22
23 } //close draw
```

FIGURE 3.15

If you typed the code exactly as above, you will notice that nothing animates. Even though there are comments, variables, and assignment operators that imply transformations, the design doesn't change. You could probably see what the problems are if you look closely at the code, but sometimes the answer isn't obvious in a sea of text. One of the best tools for debugging your code is to get a **println()** report of your custom variables. In Chapter 2, we used **println()** inside of **void mousePressed()** to get single reports of vertex positions. But, in this case we want to see how the variables will behave over time. So, we will use **println()** inside of **void draw()**.

The same syntax applies for using **println()** with custom variables:

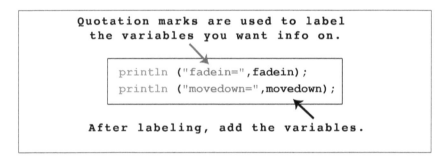

FIGURE 3.16

Add these two **println()** commands to your code from Figure 3.15 *inside* of **void draw()** after your assignment operator (but before your closing bracket). Then, run the code briefly and watch the black console print information on your two variables. If you scroll to the top of the feed you should see this:

```
fadein= 256
movedown= 100.001
fadein= 257
movedown= 100.002
fadein= 258
movedown= 100.003
```

FIGURE 3.17

This is very helpful information for figuring out why things weren't animating:

TABLE 3.1   Example Println() Results Explained

Variable Name	Println() Results	Correction
fadein	The fadein variable starts at 256 and increases by 1 over time. Thus, the opacity isn't fading in because this variable value starts fully opaque	Change the starting value of this variable to 0.
movedown	This variable is increasing as expected but the increments are very small. The animation is too tiny/slow for us to see easily.	Add a larger assignment operator value to make this animation move faster.

Exercise 3.4

a. Using the previous information, correct the two malfunctioning animations in the example (Figure 3.15).

b. Add a third animation of your choice with a new custom variable and a **println()**.

LESSON 3.5: CONSTRAIN() FOR STOPPING ANIMATIONS

Run the following program:

```
1  int shrink = 300;
2
3  void setup() {
4  size(300, 300);
5  }
6
7  void draw() {
8  background (227,234,33);
9  fill (50,124,53);
10 ellipse (150,150,shrink, shrink);
11
12 //assignment operator
13 shrink = shrink - 1;
14
15 //variable report
16 println ("shrink=",shrink);
17
18 } //close draw
```

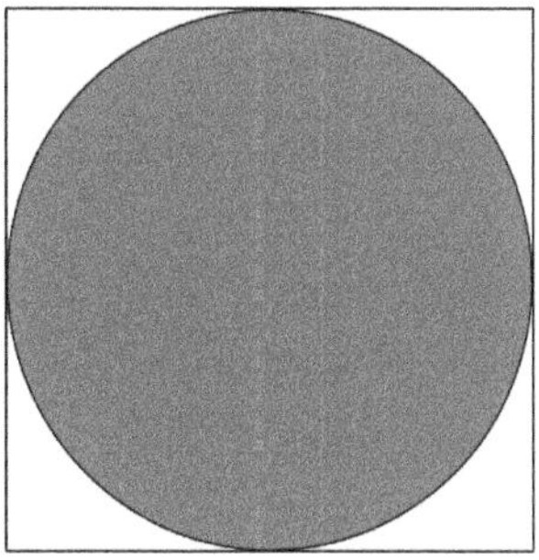

FIGURE 3.18

As you can see in the animation and the **println()** report, the animation does something unexpected. The ellipse decreases in size until the variable "shrink" hits – 1 and then the ellipse starts to grow again. This is because visualizing a negative size is not possible for growth. So, Processing defaults to the absolute value of the negative number, which in turn causes the shape to grow. But, maybe you would like the ellipse to stop shrinking when the variable hits 0? Enter the **constrain()** command.

Add this second assignment operator to the previous example (Figure 3.18) and run the code:

```
shrink = constrain(shrink, 0, 300);
```

FIGURE 3.19

As you see from the animation and the **println()**, the variable "shrink" stops at 0. Here's a syntax breakdown of **constrain()**:

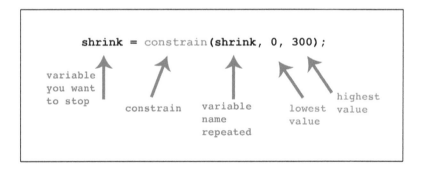

FIGURE 3.20

Run the following code:

```
1   float movedown = 25;//start at the top
2   float moveup = 275; //start at the bottom
3
4   void setup() {
5   size(300, 300);
6   }
7
8   void draw() {
9   background (40,88,20);
10  fill (250,3,197);
11  ellipse (100, movedown, 50,50);
12  fill (108,63,55);
13  ellipse (200, moveup, 50,50);
14
15  //assignment operators
16  moveup = moveup - 1;
17  moveup = constrain (moveup, 25, 275);
18  movedown = movedown + 1;
19  movedown = constrain (movedown, 25, 275);
20
21  //variable reports
22  println ("movedown=", movedown);
23  println ("moveup=", moveup);
24  } //close draw
```

FIGURE 3.21

It is important to notice that whether your variable is counting up or down, the **constrain()** syntax values are always written in this order: *lowest value, highest value.*

Exercise 3.5

Run the following starter code:

```
1  float moveright = 30;
2  float moveleft = 270;
3
4  void setup() {
5  size(300, 300);
6  }
7
8  void draw() {
9  background (155,11,47);
10 rectMode (CENTER);
11
12 fill (126, 190, 232);
13 rect (moveright, 150, 150,150);
14
15 fill (88,193,101);
16 ellipse (moveleft, 150, 150,150);
17
18 //variable reports
19 println ("moveright=",moveright);
20 println ("moveleft=",moveleft);
21
22 } //close draw
```

FIGURE 3.22

Now, animate the blue rectangle to move right and the green circle to move left at different speeds. Use **constrain()** to stop them both in the middle.

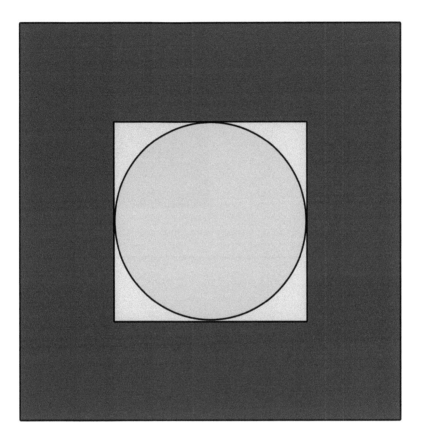

FIGURE 3.23

LESSON 3.6: RANDOM() OPPORTUNITIES

Processing has a **random()** number generator. Run the following code:

```
1   void setup() {
2   size (400,400);
3   }
4
5   void draw() {
6   background (38,93,106);
7   noStroke();
8   fill (255,255,0);
9   ellipse (random(400),random(100,300), 4,4);
10  } //close draw
```

FIGURE 3.24

You can plug **random()** into most numerical arguments. In the above example, the X and Y positions of the ellipses are randomized to the canvas's center section.

The syntax for **random()** is as follows:

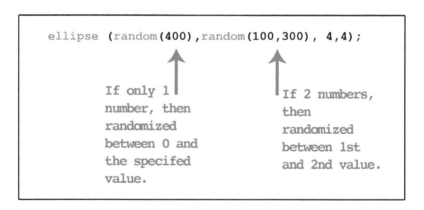

```
ellipse (random(400),random(100,300), 4,4);
```

If only 1 number, then randomized between 0 and the specifed value.

If 2 numbers, then randomized between 1st and 2nd value.

FIGURE 3.25

Animations made with **random()** look interesting when you move the **background()** into **setup()**. Try it.

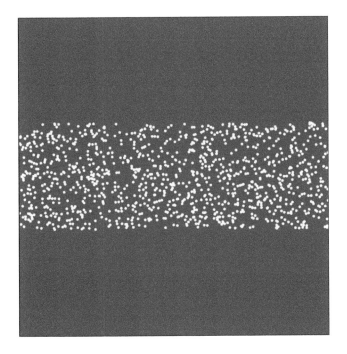

FIGURE 3.26

But remember, when your **background()** is in **setup()** then all of your animations will leave animation artifacts or "trails." Maybe you don't want this effect on *all* of your animations. We can keep the trail effect in parts of our screen and mask it away elsewhere by strategically placing shapes in **void draw()**. Run the following program:

```
1  int x = 10;
2
3  void setup() {
4  size (400,400);
5  background (38,93,106); //in setup for animation trails
6  }
7
8  void draw() {
9  noStroke();
10 fill (255,255,0);
11 ellipse (random(400),random(100,300), 4,4); //stars
12
13 //transparent filled ellipse as canvas mask
14 stroke (0,0,35);
15 strokeWeight (300);
16 fill (0,0);
17 ellipse (200,200,500,500);
18
19 //red moving ellipses
20 noStroke();
21 fill (255,0,0);
22 ellipse (x,75,35,35);
23 ellipse (x,200,35,35);
24 x = x + 1; //assignment operator
25 }//close draw
```

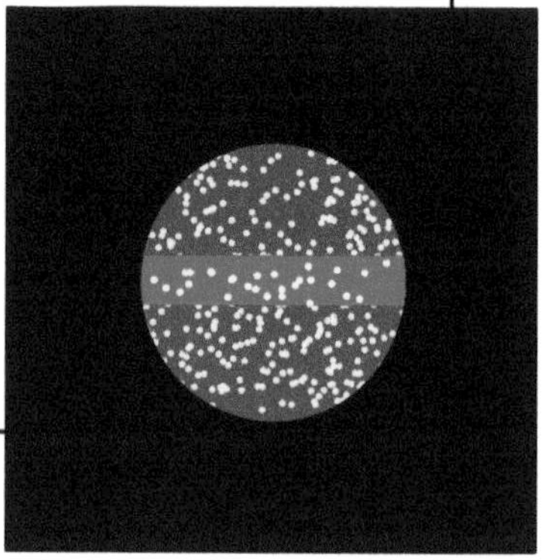

FIGURE 3.27

As you can see with the two moving red ellipses, animation artifacts only show where the **background()** is exposed.

Exercise 3.6

Code the following randomized color animation with the white background in **void setup()** and the black **rect()** in **void draw()**.

FIGURE 3.28

LESSON 3.7: AUTOMATED ROTATIONS

Remember the mouse responsive animations using **rotate()** from Chapter 2? Now, we will automate these rotations with a custom variable. Run the following program:

```
1  float pinwheel1 = 0;
2
3  void setup(){
4  size (450,300);
5  }
6
7  void draw(){
8  background (0);
9
10 //pinwheel handle
11 strokeWeight(1);
12 stroke(255);
13 line (100,100,100,300);
14
15 pushMatrix(); //start temporary change to the grid system
16 translate (100,100); //move 0,0 position to 100,100
17 rotate (radians(pinwheel1)); //rotate in radians w/variable
18
19 //shapes to rotate
20 strokeWeight (10);
21 stroke (255,24,0,100);
22 ellipse (50,0,100,20);
23 ellipse (-50,0,100,20);
24 ellipse (0,-50,20,100);
25 ellipse (0,50,20,100);
26
27 pinwheel1 = pinwheel1 + 1; //assignment operator animates
28 popMatrix(); //end pixel grid transformation
29
30 //circle design overlay on pinwheel
31 fill (255);
32 noStroke();
33 ellipse (100,100,25,25);
34 }//close draw
```

FIGURE 3.29

Most of this should feel familiar except for the additional use of a custom variable inserted into **radians()** – which causes the automated rotation. However, the x and y vertices positions of the four ellipses might be a bit confusing because of the temporary movement of the 0,0 position for the grid system. Here's a detailed diagram to understand the argument positions for each ellipse. It is helpful to turn off the assignment operator to see each ellipse in its starting position.

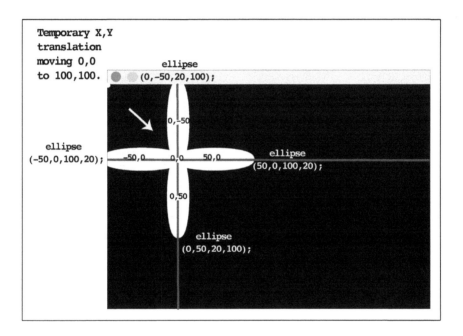

FIGURE 3.30

Exercise 3.7

Add two more pinwheels to the previous program (Figure 3.30), a yellow one in the middle that spins backwards, and a blue one on the far right that spins forward and faster than the other two.

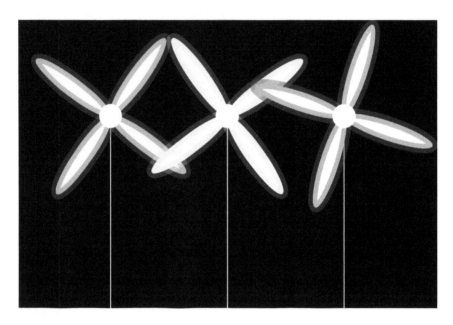

FIGURE 3.31

PROJECT: AUTOMATED ENVIRONMENT

Create a new environment. If your last project was outside then make an indoor environment (or, the reverse). This time add automated animations with custom variables that change position, size, and color. Consider also using **mousePressed()**, **mouseX**, and **mouseY** to enhance your automated project with interactivity as well. See project examples in the downloads folder available from the publisher's website.

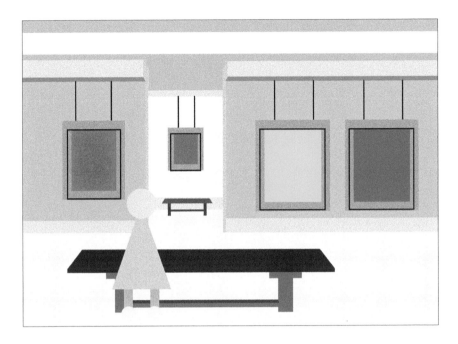

FIGURE 3.32   Student project example: animated art project. (Printed with permission from Nalani Patterson.)

FIGURE 3.33   Student project example: animated art project. (Printed with permission from Liam Nolan).

CHAPTER 4

Animated Collages

FIGURE 4.1   Student project example: animated collage. (Printed with permission from Maiah Cooper.)

In Chapters 1–3, we programmed our designs with only the shape commands available from Processing. In this chapter, we will import external images such as photographs, digital drawings, scans, and/or internet clip art. This strategy will allow for more detailed project designs using unique textures, complex patterns, and non-standard shapes.

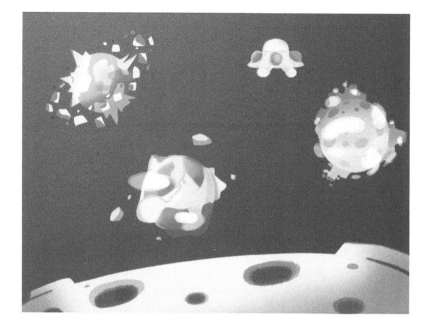

FIGURE 4.2 Student project example: animated collage. (Printed with permission from Claire Bridges.)

LESSON 4.1 PREPARING AND IMPORTING IMAGERY

Before we import our images, we need to optimize them for Processing. The following table is an overview on preparing images for use in Processing.

TABLE 4.1 Preparing Images

Guideline	Explanation
Dots Per Inch (DPI)	An image quality of 70 – 100 DPI is a good resolution for computer graphics. Higher image resolutions may slow your Processing projects down. Images taken from the internet are usually within this DPI range. If you scan or create your own custom images on the computer, you usually can specify their DPI. See your particular device/software for more information.
Aspect Ratio	This is the width and height of your images in pixels (aka size). It is usually best to keep your image imports the same size or smaller than your Processing project's canvas.
File Formats	.jpg and .png are the most common file formats. .png allows for invisible backgrounds and transparencies.

(Continued)

TABLE 4.1 (Continued) Preparing Images

Guideline	Explanation
Sources	You can use digital imagery from online or your own archives. If your images are too high in resolution, the wrong file format, or need design edits, then adjust them in a photo-editing program. There are plenty of retail and free applications/websites available for editing imagery. Keywords when searching for editors: image converter, background eraser, photo editor, and photo manipulation.

For the following lessons and exercises, please download the folder: "Chapter 4 Lesson Imagery" from the publisher's website. Here, you will find the following four .png files at a resolution of 72 DPI and a size of 200 × 200 pixels. All four of these images have invisible backgrounds. If you are unable to download these images, then find similar images and use the same file names:

Four images to work with:

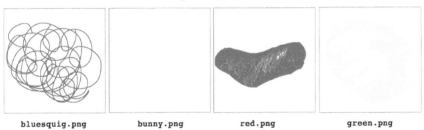

bluesquig.png   bunny.png   red.png   green.png

FIGURE 4.3

Images are external to Processing and need to be imported in a particular way. In order to make them available for use in a Processing sketch, we need to create a data folder *inside* of our Processing sketch folder.

To do this:

- First, create a new Processing file
- Go to "Sketch" on the title bar and click "Show Sketchbook Folder"

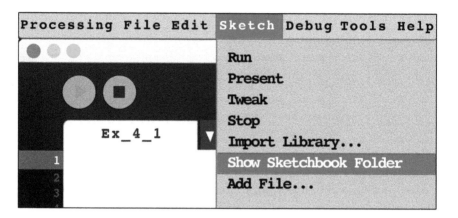

FIGURE 4.4

Next:

- Create a new folder inside of the Processing sketchbook folder and name it: *data* (this folder must have this exact name)
- Place the four .png photos inside of the data folder

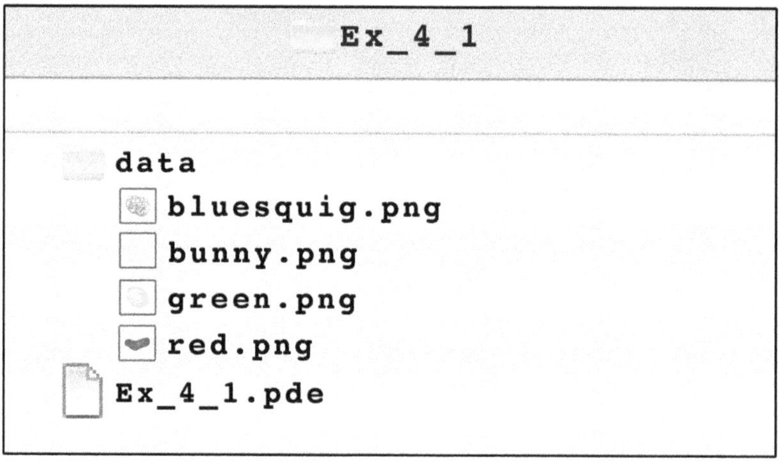

Ex_4_1
data
bluesquig.png
bunny.png
green.png
red.png
Ex_4_1.pde

FIGURE 4.5

It is critical that your images are placed *inside* of the data folder. If you run an image-based Processing project and your photos are not in the correct place, then your program might crash. If this happens with future projects, quit Processing and verify your files are in the project's data folder.

Once your images are in the right place, the next step is to write the code to display them. The following example (Figure 4.6) outlines the three steps needed to display an image on the Processing canvas. Pay special attention to the code and comments of this example. There are new types of variables, commands, and syntax. When you run the program (and, if you have no typos and your data folder is in place) then the following green image should appear.

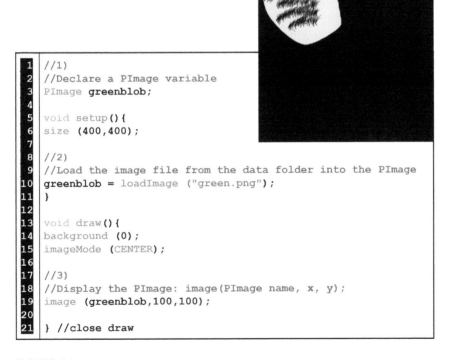

```
1  //1)
2  //Declare a PImage variable
3  PImage greenblob;
4
5  void setup(){
6  size (400,400);
7
8  //2)
9  //Load the image file from the data folder into the PImage
10 greenblob = loadImage ("green.png");
11 }
12
13 void draw(){
14 background (0);
15 imageMode (CENTER);
16
17 //3)
18 //Display the PImage: image(PImage name, x, y);
19 image (greenblob,100,100);
20
21 } //close draw
```

FIGURE 4.6

TABLE 4.2   Programming Steps for Displaying Images

Step	Explanation
(1)	In order to access an image, a PImage variable first needs to be declared at the top of your code above **void setup()** and **void draw()**. As with other custom variables, you can name **PImage** variables most anything.
(2)	In **void setup()**, we load the images from the data folder into the PImage variables. It is very important that you type the file name in quotes exactly as it reads in the data folder (including .jpg or .png). Also, note that images are loaded in **void setup()** to free up CPU usage.
(3)	In **void draw()**, we tell the computer where to display the images. In the previous example (Figure 4.6), there are three arguments inside of the image() command: image (*PImage name, x position, y position*); Also, note that using the command: **imageMode (CENTER);** before **image()** will anchor your x and y positions at the center.

Exercise 4.1

To keep your work consistent with the examples and exercises in this chapter, use the following names for the **PImage** variables: *lines, rabbit, redblob,* and *greenblob.* For this exercise, add onto the previous example (Figure 4.6), so that all four of the .png images are displayed in all four corners like this:

FIGURE 4.7

LESSON 4.2: MOVING IMAGES

As with Processing shapes, imported images can be animated in a variety of ways using custom variables. Create a new Processing sketch, add the data folder, and run the following code to see these two images move across the screen.

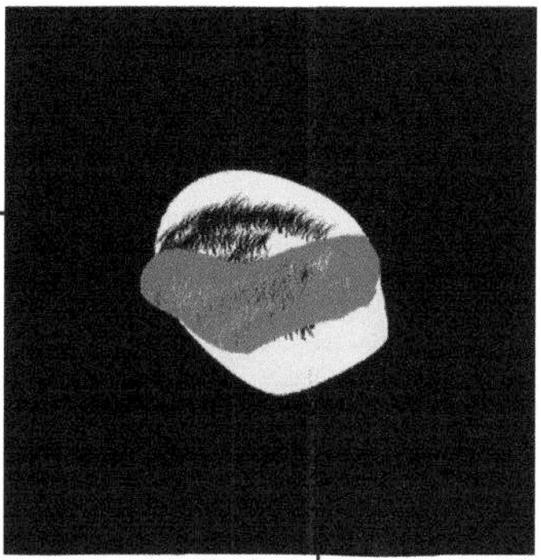

```
1   //image variables
2   PImage greenblob;
3   PImage redblob;
4
5   //movement variables (starting offscreen)
6   float moveright = -100;
7   float moveleft = 500;
8
9   void setup(){
10  size (400,400);
11
12  //images from the data folder are loaded into the variables
13  greenblob = loadImage ("green.png");
14  redblob = loadImage ("red.png");
15  }
16
17  void draw(){
18  background (0);
19  imageMode (CENTER);
20
21  //images are displayed with variables in their x positions
22  image (greenblob, moveright, 200);
23  image (redblob, moveleft, 200);
24
25  //assignment operators animate & constrain images
26  moveright = moveright + .75;
27  moveleft = moveleft - 1;
28  moveright = constrain (moveright,-100,200);
29  moveleft = constrain (moveleft,200,500);
30  }
```

FIGURE 4.8

Exercise 4.2

In the previous example (Figure 4.8), half of the work is completed for this exercise. Now, adjust this code so that:

a. All four images start off-screen on all four sides.

b. All four images move to the center of the canvas at different speeds.

c. All four images stop in the center.

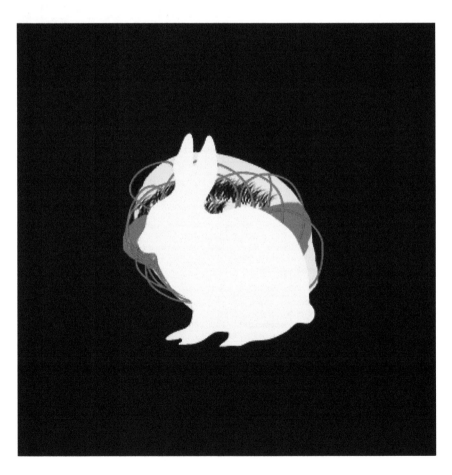

FIGURE 4.9

LESSON 4.3: FADING AND COLORING IMAGES USING TINT()

We can colorize and change the opacity of an image using the **tint()** command. The **tint()** command works similarly to **fill()** and **stroke()**, however, the color results are not always the same.

TABLE 4.3   Tint() Overview

Example	Visual Result
tint (0);	Black overlay
tint (100);	Gray overlay
tint (255);	White overlay – but *not visible*
noTint();	Fully opaque and original image color
tint (255, 0);	Fully transparent
tint (255, 100);	Some transparency, no color change
tint (255, 0, 0);	Red image overlays
tint (0, 255, 0);	Green image overlays
tint (0, 0, 255);	Blue image overlays

Create a new Processing sketch, add the data folder, and run the following code:

```
1   PImage greenblob;
2   PImage redblob;
3   PImage rabbit;
4   PImage lines;
5
6   void setup(){
7   size (400,400);
8   greenblob = loadImage ("green.png");
9   redblob = loadImage ("red.png");
10  rabbit = loadImage ("bunny.png");
11  lines = loadImage ("bluesquig.png");
12  }
13
14  void draw(){
15  background (242,97,12);
16  imageMode (CENTER);
17
18  tint (0); //tints all images that follow
19  image (greenblob,100,100);
20  image (lines, 100, 300);
21  image (redblob, 300, 100);
22
23  noTint(); //stops tinting
24  image (rabbit,300, 300);
25
26  } //close draw
```

FIGURE 4.10

To see how **tint()** works, play around with the previous example by changing the **tint()** for each image. Also, note that because **void draw()** is always running, a **tint()** command to one image will impact all of the images in a project. If you don't want certain images tinted, then use the **noTint()** command before them.

Exercise 4.3

In the following starter code (Figure 4.11), the bunny fades out and the far left blob turns red when you click the mouse. To see this in action, create a new Processing sketch, add the data folder, and run the code. After you get it working, program the following additions:

a. Make the blue, squiggly line start transparent and fade in with mouse clicks.

b. Make the far right blob start black and turn green with mouse clicks.

```
1   //image variables
2   PImage greenblob;
3   PImage redblob;
4   PImage rabbit;
5   PImage lines;
6
7   //tint variables
8   int rgb = 0;
9   int fadeout = 255;
10
11  void setup(){
12  size (400,300);
13
14  greenblob = loadImage ("green.png");
15  redblob = loadImage ("red.png");
16  rabbit = loadImage ("bunny.png");
17  lines = loadImage ("bluesquig.png");
18  } //close setup
19
20  void draw(){
21  background (255);
22  imageMode (CENTER);
23
24  tint (rgb,0,0);
25  image (greenblob,100,150);
26
27  noTint();
28  image (redblob,300,150);
29  image (lines,200,150);
30
31  tint (255,fadeout);
32  image (rabbit,200,150);
33  } //close draw
34
35  void mousePressed(){
36  rgb = rgb + 35;
37  fadeout = fadeout - 30;
38  } //close mousePressed
```

FIGURE 4.11

LESSON 4.4: RESIZING IMAGES & MULTIPLES

Using lots of images in a Processing project requires extra CPU power and this can potentially bog down your program. But, the detailed design opportunities available from imported images makes this challenge worth overcoming. Resizing images can be particularly burdensome on CPU usage but there are workarounds. The first workaround is to correct the size of your images *before* you import them into Processing. However, for a variety of reasons this option may not work for you. The following table shows two alternate methods for resizing images in Processing.

TABLE 4.4   Image Resizing Overview

Method	Outcome	Code Example

(1) Resize your images in **void setup()** with the **.resize** command	This method is far less burdening on CPU usage. However, if you want to resize several copies of the same image then you have to declare, load, resize, and display each copy.	```
		PImage rabbit1;
		PImage rabbit2;
		
		void setup(){
		
		rabbit1 = loadImage ("bunny.png");
		rabbit1.resize (25,25);
		
		rabbit2 = loadImage ("bunny.png");
		rabbit2.resize (75,75);
		}
		
		void draw(){
		imageMode (CENTER);
		image (rabbit1,20,20);
		image (rabbit2,60,60);
		}
		``

(2) Resize your images in **void draw()** by adding a 4th and 5th argument to the **image()** command	Most convenient, there are no extra commands needed. Also, less lines of code are needed if you want to resize several copies of the same image. This method allows for scaled animations. However, this method might slow your program down so use it sparingly.	```
		PImage rabbit;
		
		void setup(){
		
		rabbit = loadImage ("bunny.png");
		}
		
		void draw(){
		imageMode (CENTER);
		image (rabbit,20,20,25,25);
		image (rabbit,60,60,75,75);
		}
		``

If you don't need to resize images but you do want to display several copies of the same image, then method (2) without the 4th and 5th arguments in **image()** will work best.

Exercise 4.4

The following program animates the red bunny to grow. Start a new Processing sketch, add the data folder, and run the code. Afterwards, make the green bunny shrink until it gets to 25 × 25 pixels.

```
1   //image variable
2   PImage rabbit;
3
4   //size variable
5   int grow = 25;
6
7   void setup(){
8   size (400,400);
9   rabbit = loadImage ("bunny.png");
10  }
11
12  void draw(){
13  background (0);
14  imageMode (CENTER);
15
16  tint (255,0,0); //red bunny
17  image (rabbit,120,200,grow,grow);
18
19  tint (0,255,0); //green bunny
20  image (rabbit,280,200,250,250);
21
22  //assignment operators
23  grow = grow + 1;
24  grow = constrain(grow,25,250);
25  } //close draw
```

FIGURE 4.12

LESSON 4.5: CONSTRAINING MOUSE MOVEMENTS

Imported images can easily be programmed to respond to mouse movements. Just drop **mouseX** or **mouseY** into one of the **image()** command's arguments and watch things transform. But, what if you want to limit the **mouseX** or **mouseY** animations to a certain range? Ideally, you would apply the **constrain()** function directly to them. This kind of works but is a bit sloppy. To see for yourself, create a new Processing sketch, add the data folder, and run the following code:

```
1  PImage rabbit;
2
3  void setup(){
4  size (600,600);
5  rabbit = loadImage ("bunny.png");
6  }
7
8  void draw(){
9  background (253,30,222);
10
11 //transparent box
12 rectMode (CENTER);
13 stroke (255);
14 fill (0,0);
15 rect (300,300,400,400);
16
17 //rabbit and ellipse
18 imageMode (CENTER);
19 noStroke();
20 fill (255);
21 ellipse (mouseX,300,300,300);//mouseX moves the ellipse
22 tint(0,255,0);
23 image (rabbit,mouseX,300); //mouseX moves the image
24
25 //failed assignment operator
26 //mouse movements are too fluid to be cleanly constrained
27 mouseX = constrain (mouseX,250,350);
28
29 } //close draw
```

FIGURE 4.13   The bunny/ellipse won't stay within the white lines.

As you can see, the boundaries are not very clean for keeping the bunny/ellipse inside of the white lines. The mouse is hard to control with exact precision. But, we can fix this by assigning a limited range of **mouseX** movements to a custom variable. Create a new Processing sketch, add the data folder, and run the following code:

```
//image variable
PImage rabbit;

//variable added to constrain mouse movements
float a = 300;

void setup(){
size (600,600);
rabbit = loadImage ("bunny.png");
}

void draw(){
background (253,30,222);

//white box outline
rectMode (CENTER);
stroke (255);
fill (0,0);
rect (300,300,400,400);

//rabbit and ellipse
imageMode (CENTER);
noStroke();
fill (255);
ellipse (a,300,300,300); //"a" substitutes for mouseX
tint(0,255,0);
image (rabbit,a,300); //"a" substitutes for mouseX

//the assignment operator constrains "a"
//to mouseX values in a limited range
a = constrain (mouseX,250,350);

//report on variable "a" and mouseX
println ("mouseX=", mouseX, "a=", a);

} //close draw
```

FIGURE 4.14

In this revised version of **constrain()**, a range of **mouseX** values are assigned to the custom variable "a". A custom variable is more controllable than the mouse and so the boundaries stay tight. Move the mouse and watch the **println()** report to see for yourself.

Exercise 4.5

Add onto the previous example (Figure 4.14), so that the ellipse/bunny can also move up and down but only within the white lines.

LESSON 4.6: VOID KEY PRESSED() WITH IMAGE ROTATIONS

In Chapters 2 and 3, we used the **rotate()** command to spin Processing shapes. Now, we will apply the **rotate()** command to imported images by pressing a key. Create a new Processing sketch, add the data folder, and run the following program:

```
1  //Press any key to see animation.
2
3  // image variable
4  PImage lines;
5
6  //spin variable
7  int spin = 0;
8
9  void setup(){
10 size (500,500);
11 lines = loadImage ("bluesquig.png");
12 }
13
14 void draw(){
15 background (255);
16 imageMode (CENTER);
17
18 pushMatrix();
19 translate (250,250); //put 0,0 in center of canvas
20 rotate (radians(spin));
21 noTint();
22 image (lines,0,0); //1st image rotation
23 image (lines,100,100);//2nd image rotation offset by 100
24 popMatrix();
25
26 } //close draw
27
28 void keyPressed(){
29
30 //assignment operator
31 spin = spin + 10;
32
33 } //close void keyPressed
```

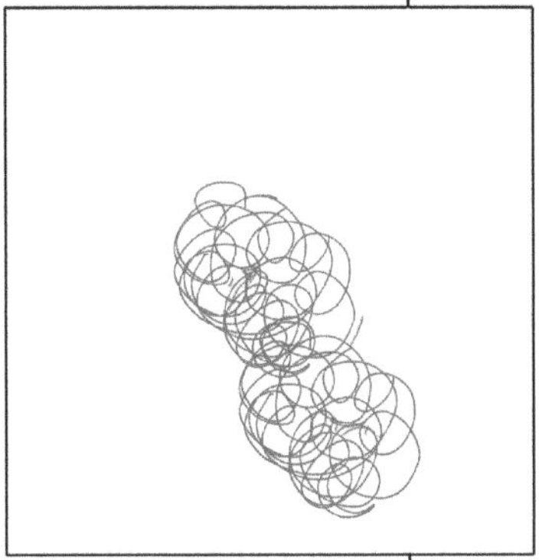

FIGURE 4.15

As you can see, **void keyPressed()** works like **void mousePressed()** but with any key pressed.

Exercise 4.6

Using the code from the previous example (Figure 4.15), add 2 more of the same image in the same place. But this time, make the 2 additions green and spin them counterclockwise when a key is pressed.

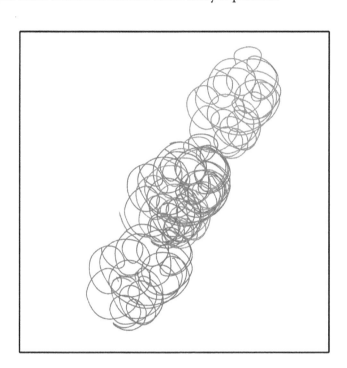

FIGURE 4.16   Positioning after several keys pressed.

Side note: Some interesting animations can result when you move your **background()** into **void setup()**.

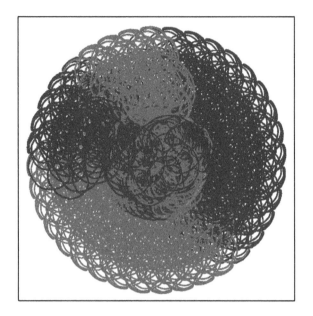

FIGURE 4.17

LESSON 4.7: CREATE FONTS

When adding text to your projects, you may want to customize your fonts. Processing has a built-in tool that allows you to create custom fonts for your projects.

Create a new Processing sketch, navigate to "Tools" and select "Create Font".

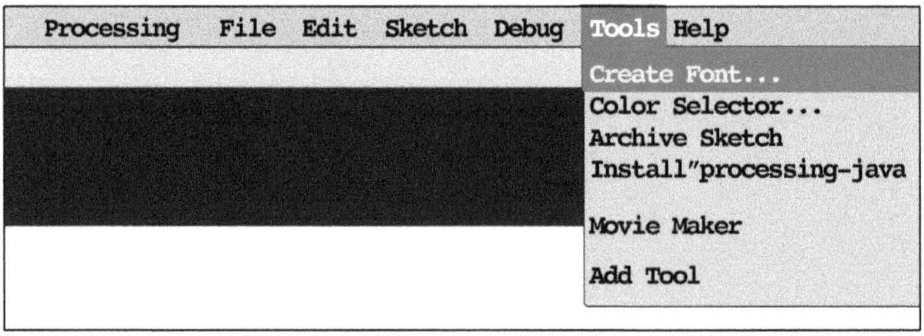

FIGURE 4.18

Next, select the font type "Calibri" and a size of 50…

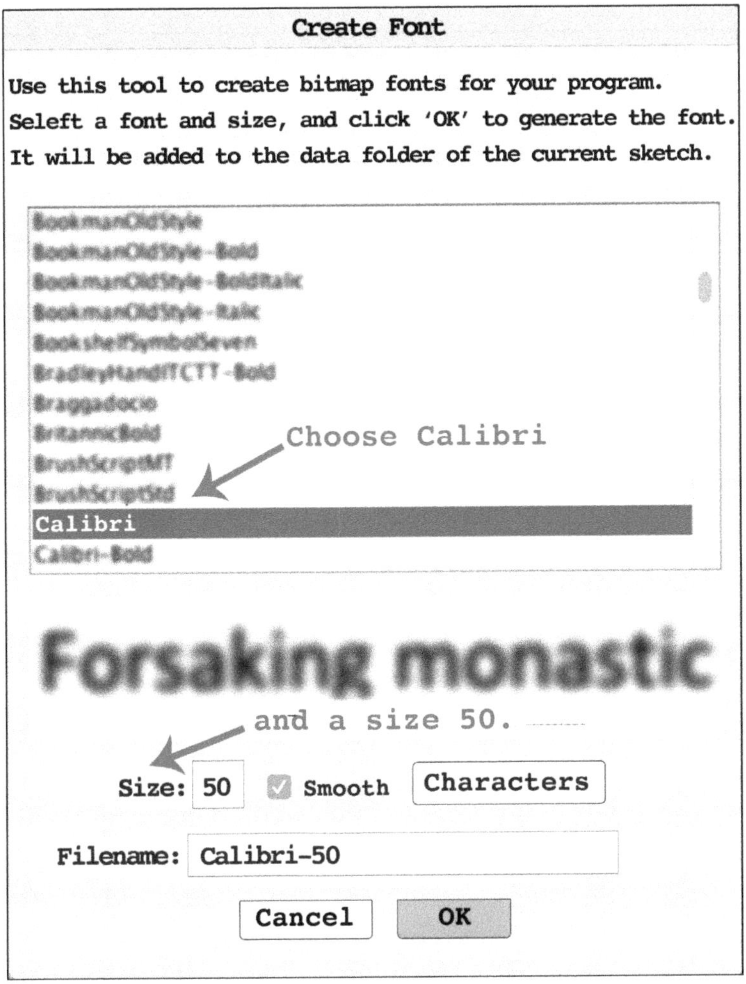

FIGURE 4.19

If you look at your Processing sketch folder, you should see the newly created font inside of the data folder:

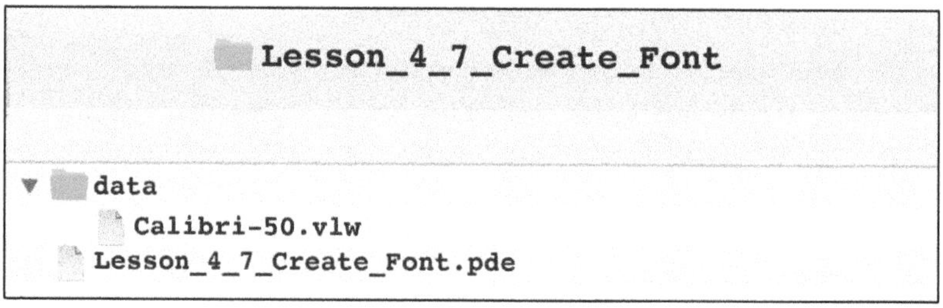

Lesson_4_7_Create_Font

▼ data
    Calibri-50.vlw
    Lesson_4_7_Create_Font.pde

FIGURE 4.20

Now, we will program the font to display. Run, the following code:

```
1  //declare a PFont variable
2  PFont myfont;
3
4  void setup () {
5  size (500,200);
6
7  //load the font file from the data folder into the variable
8  myfont = loadFont("Calibri-50.vlw");
9  }
10
11 void draw () {
12 background (205,211,34);
13 fill(31,93,25);
14
15 //call the font
16 textFont(myfont);
17
18 //write your text in quotes and specify its position
19 text("This is the Calibri font.",25,100);
20
21 }//close draw
```

This is the Calibri font.

FIGURE 4.21

As you can see, there are similarities between displaying a custom font and an imported image. PFonts variables are declared at the top, and also initialized in **void setup()**. However, in **void draw()**, things are little different because you use two commands: **textfont()** and **text()**. For a review of the X, Y anchor positions of **text()**, see Lesson 2.7.

Exercise 4.7

Start a new Processing sketch, create an "AdobeArabic-Italic" font at a size of 48, and run the following animated program:

```
1  PFont myfont;
2
3  int x = -350;//starts text off screen
4
5  void setup () {
6  size (700,200);
7  myfont = loadFont("AdobeArabic-Italic-48.vlw");
8  }
9
10 void draw () {
11 background (32,17,131);
12 fill(254,125,25);
13
14 textFont(myfont);
15 text("My favorite things are...", x, 75);
16
17 //assignment operators
18 x = x + 1;
19 x = constrain(x, -350,100);
20
21 }//close draw
```

FIGURE 4.22

Next, add onto this program with the following:

a. Create a new font of your choice.

b. Finish the sentence, "My favorite things are…" with a new text line in a different color that slides in from the right side and stops under the first text line.

LESSON 4.8: PROJECT OPTIMIZATION AND NOSMOOTH()

The lessons in this chapter provide several tools for creating dynamic projects with imported images. But, it is important to remember that using lots of images can bog your program down. To optimize your image-based projects, keep an eye on the DPI resolution and size of each image you import. If you find that your animations aren't behaving as you expected, run a **println()** report on your variables to get more information. Finally, if you find that your image-based project is running slow or the animations look jerky then use the command **noSmooth()**. By default, Processing automatically smooths the edges of images by 3 pixels. Here's a comparison of the built-in smoothing versus running the **noSmooth()** command:

FIGURE 4.23

Sometimes this built-in smoothing really helps with the look of images displayed in Processing and sometimes it isn't detectable. But, if you have several imported images, this smoothing feature might slow your animations down. If you have a heavily image-based project then try adding **noSmooth()** inside of **void setup()** to optimize your animations. To see this principle in action, download the project examples for this chapter from the publisher's website and compare how they run with **noSmooth()** turned on and off.

PROJECT: ANIMATED AND INTERACTIVE COLLAGE

Using the programming strategies from Chapters 1 to 4, create a visually integrated and animated collage with several imported images. Make sure that there are animations that are both interactive and automated. Consider making an abstracted portrait or another new environment. Also, note that it can be helpful to make a project plan and prepare your images (Table 4.1) before you begin programming. See project examples in the download folder available from the publisher's website.

FIGURE 4.24   Student project example: animated collage. (Printed with permission from Natalie Cote.)

FIGURE 4.25   Student project example: animated collage. (Printed with permission from Sierra Gillingham.)

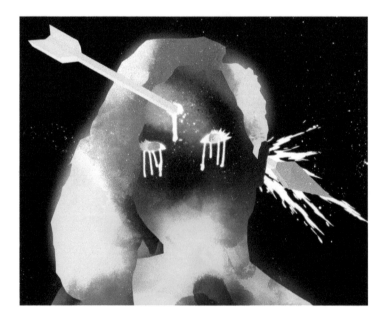

FIGURE 4.26   Student project example: animated collage. (Printed with permission from Cianan Veltz.)

CHAPTER 5

Conditional Interactions and Rollovers

FIGURE 5.1   Student project example: rollover animation. (Printed with permission from Gillian Probert.)

In this chapter, we will program conditions for triggering animations and events. For example, in Figure 5.1, when the user moves the mouse, the marble follows it down the ramp. In Figure 5.2, when the mouse hovers over the doorbell, the program displays the words, "ring, ring." The techniques in this chapter are the foundations of building complex projects intricately responsive to user input.

FIGURE 5.2   Student project example: rollover animation. (Printed with permission from Olivia Madarang.)

LESSON 5.1: CONDITIONAL STATEMENTS AND RELATIONAL OPERATORS

In order to program a sequence of interactive choices and events, we will use **if** statements. These **if** statements contain conditions that the computer verifies as either true or false. Depending on the answers to a conditional **if** statement, the computer will execute specific code commands or ignore them. For the projects in this book, some common conditions and events we will implement are shown in Table 5.1.

TABLE 5.1   Conditions and Events

Condition	Event
if the mouse is hovering over a certain region...	then trigger an animation.
if the mouse is clicked in a certain position...	then load the next screen.
if a certain key is pressed...	then move a character image.
if a variable becomes larger than a certain value...	then reset this variable.

To program these events, our conditional tests will be written as numerical statements. We will make comparisons to check things like the position of the mouse or the value of a variable. If the computer program verifies that a certain numerical statement is true then it will execute the code. In order to write these expressions, we need to use relational operators.

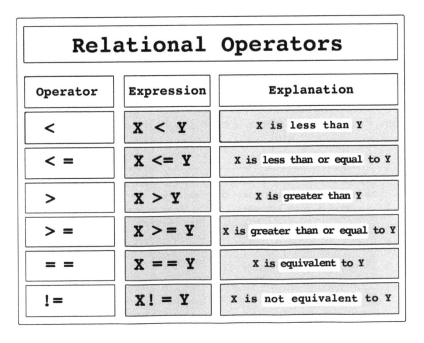

Relational Operators

Operator	Expression	Explanation
<	X < Y	X is less than Y
< =	X <= Y	X is less than or equal to Y
>	X > Y	X is greater than Y
> =	X >= Y	X is greater than or equal to Y
= =	X == Y	X is equivalent to Y
! =	X! = Y	X is not equivalent to Y

FIGURE 5.3

To see this all put together, run the following program:

```
1   void setup() {
2   size (300,300);
3   }
4
5   void draw() {
6   background (103,142,58);
7
8   //if mouseX is larger than 150...
9   if (mouseX > 150) {
10
11  //then execute this code
12  fill ( 191,122,2);
13  ellipse (150,150,250,250);
14  }
15
16  println ("mouseX",mouseX);
17
18  }//close draw
```

FIGURE 5.4

Conditional statements allow computer programs to make decisions on whether or not to execute lines of code. In the previous example, when the mouse is on the left, the condition becomes false and the ellipse is not drawn. But, when the mouse is moved right beyond 150, the condition becomes true and the ellipse is drawn.

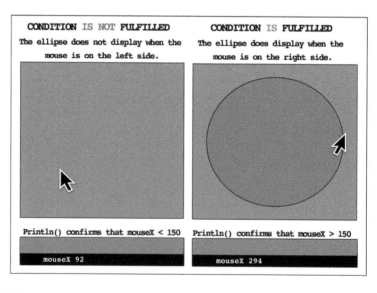

FIGURE 5.5

It is important to note the new syntax and formatting of conditional statements. The word **if** is followed by a test condition in parenthesis. The code you wish to execute is then written in between curly brackets. As you can see, the semicolon *does not* close every line of code in a program. Also, if you miss a bracket pairing then your code will break. Finally, remember that the commands inside of the **if** statement's curly brackets *will only be executed if the condition is fulfilled (true)*. Once the code is executed, the program moves on and exits the **if** statement.

Exercise 5.1

On a 300 × 300 canvas, program the following rollover so that the yellow ellipse only displays when the mouse cursor is on the upper half of the screen.

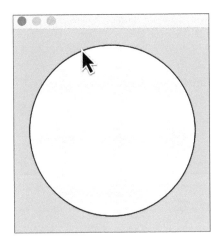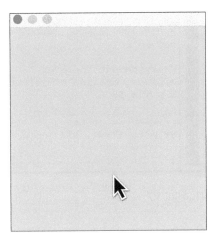

FIGURE 5.6

LESSON 5.2: CONDITIONAL STATEMENTS
WITH CUSTOM VARIABLES

Combining conditional statements with custom variables is the real pow-
erhouse of programming. Run the following code of a looping rectangle:

```
1   int x = -150; //x position starts off screen
2
3   void setup () {
4   size (400,200);
5   }
6
7   void draw() {
8   rectMode (CENTER);
9   background (255,30,3);
10  fill (207,255,28);
11
12  rect (x,100,100,100);
13
14  if (x > 500){ //if the variable "x" is greater than 500
15  x = - 150; //then reset "x" to -150
16  }
17
18  //assignment operator
19  //placed outside of if{} for continuous animation
20  x = x + 5;
21
22  //variable report
23  println ("x=", x);
24
25  } //close draw
```

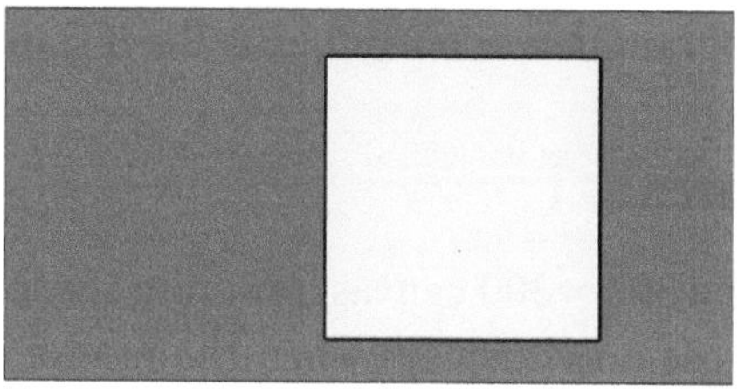

FIGURE 5.7

In the previous example, when the variable x gets to 500, it is reset to
−150 and the program exits the **if** statement. But, x's assignment operator
(x = x + 5) brings x's value right back up to 500. So, the cycle repeats causing the conditional test to become true over and over again, thus creating
a looping animation.

You may have also noticed that the condition (x == 500), has two equal
signs but the variable reset (x = −150) has only one. This is an important
syntax detail.

```
// A double equal sign is a question of equality.
// Example: is x equivalent to 500?
if(x == 500){


// A single equal sign assigns a value.
   Example: x is -150.
x = -150;
```

FIGURE 5.8

The looping logic shown in this example is the underlying principle for creating many interesting animations such as scrolling image backgrounds. In the project examples download packet associated with this chapter (available on the publisher's website), there is an annotated model of a scrolling image background.

Exercise 5.2

Using the following starter code:

a. Make the green ellipse travel up while turning black.

b. Reset the ellipse's position and color every time it goes off-screen.

```
1   int y = 250;
2
3   void setup () {
4   size (150,300);
5   }
6
7   void draw() {
8   background (196,3,255);
9   fill (0,y,0);
10  ellipse (75,y,75,75);
11
12  }//close draw
```

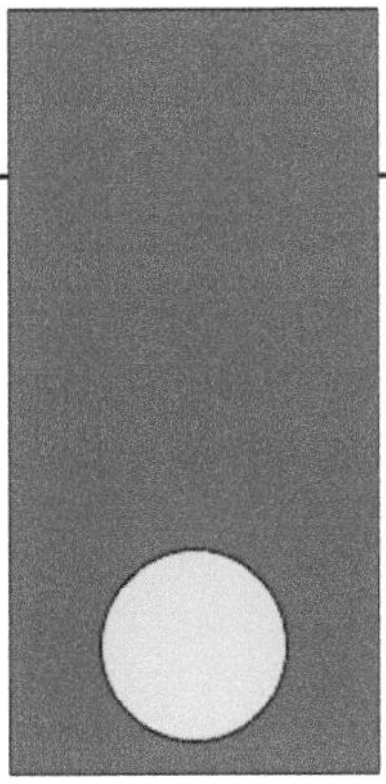

FIGURE 5.9

LESSON 5.3: AND vs. OR

In more complex projects, you will have several conditional statements. Conditionals offer a weaved tapestry of dynamic interaction but must be programmed carefully. Multiple logics can overlap or even conflict with each other. To see this in action, run the following program:

```
1   void setup () {
2   size (300,200);
3   }
4
5   void draw () {
6   background (0);
7
8   //line boundaries
9   stroke (255);
10  line (100,0,100,height);
11  line (200,0,200,height);
12
13  //draw red ellipse when mouseX is less than 200
14  if (mouseX < 200) {
15  fill (255,0,0,100);
16  ellipse (100,100,200,200);
17  }
18
19  //draw blue ellipse when mouseX is greater than 100
20  if (mouseX > 100) {
21  fill (0,0,255,100);
22  ellipse (200,100,200,200);
23  }
24
25  println ("mouseX=", mouseX);
26  }//close draw
```

FIGURE 5.10

In the previous example, each **if** statement has its own condition. But, they also have overlapping conditions. Consequently, they both can be executed at the same time (in certain circumstances).

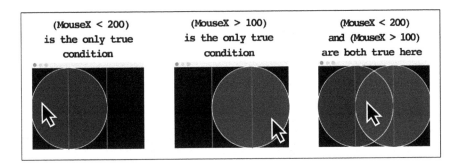

FIGURE 5.11

In many projects, having conditional logic with multiple events occurring at the same time will be desirable (or at least not an issue). But, sometimes you may want events triggered independently and not overlapping. We can extend the **if** structure to allow for a *choice* between two or more conditions. To do this, we will use **else if**. In the previous code example (Figure 5.10), replace the second **if** statement with **else if** like this:

```
else if (mouseX > 100) {
```

FIGURE 5.12

You will now see that only one ellipse can display at a time. Even though these two conditionals have overlapping regions, the program gives priority to the **if** condition over the **else if** condition. The **else if** condition only becomes active when the mouse is beyond their overlapping sections. In Processing, every conditional statement opens with one (and only one) use of the word **if**. However, you can extend an **if** statement with as many **else if** choices as needed. Also, if you need a condition that specifies *everything else* not specified in the previous **if** or **else if** statements then you can use one **else** at the end of your conditional statement. At first this may seem confusing but the more you use conditional logic, the clearer it will become. To see **if, else if** and **else** structures working together, run the following example:

```
1   int count = 0; //incremental variable starts at 0
2
3   void setup () {
4   size (200,200);
5   }
6
7   void draw() {
8   background (232,101,28);
9   triangle (0,200,100,100,200,200);
10  triangle (0,0,100,100,200,0);
11
12  //assignment operator increases the "count" variable by 1
13  count = count + 1;
14
15  //blue
16  if (count <= 50) { //is "count" less than or equal to 50?
17  fill (31,90,255); //if yes then the fill is blue.
18  } //exit when the count becomes 51
19
20  //aqua
21  else if (count <= 100) { //otherwise, is "count" 51-100?
22  fill (25,235,187); //if yes then the fill is aqua
23  } //exit when the count becomes 101
24
25  //magenta
26  else if (count <= 150) { //otherwise, is "count" 101-150?
27  fill (232,28,130); //if yes then the fill is magenta
28  }//exit when the count becomes 151
29
30  else { //if every prior condition is no longer true then
31  count = 0; //reset the count variable
32  }
33
34  //variable report
35  println ("count=",count);
36
37  }//close draw
```

FIGURE 5.13

In the previous example, four conditions execute four different outcomes depending on the value of the variable, "count". The first three conditions control the color of the two triangles while the final **else** condition resets the "count" variable to 0 (which starts the whole sequence over again). This example is a good model for observing the syntax of complex conditional statements using **if, else if**, and **else** structures. It is imperative to understand how these conditional statements and keywords work together in order to move forward with more advanced programming.

TABLE 5.2   Conditional Statements Overview

Keyword	Placement & Instances	Condition Specifications	Format

if	The keyword **if** is always required, always used first, and only used once per each conditional statement.	A testable condition is always specified inside of parentheses after **if**.	**if** (condition) {
			code to execute;
			}

else if	The keyword **else if** is optional and used as many times as needed after **if**.	A testable condition is always specified inside of parentheses after **else if**.	**else if** (condition) {
			code to execute;
			}

else	The keyword **else** is optional, only used once, and always last in the sequence.
	It can follow **if** or **else if**.
		No condition needs to be specified. The keyword **else** refers to all conditions not previously specified by any conjoining **if** or **else if**(s).	**else** {
			code to execute;
			}

Exercise 5.3

Do *not* run the following code examples right away. First, see if you can guess what color the ellipses will be by examining the conditional statements. Then run the code to check your answers.

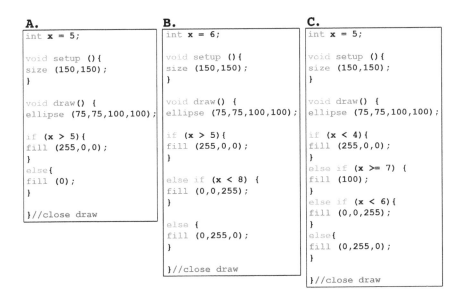

A.
```
int x = 5;

void setup () {
size (150,150);
}

void draw() {
ellipse (75,75,100,100);

if (x > 5) {
fill (255,0,0);
}
else {
fill (0);
}

}//close draw
```

B.
```
int x = 6;

void setup () {
size (150,150);
}

void draw() {
ellipse (75,75,100,100);

if (x > 5) {
fill (255,0,0);
}

else if (x < 8) {
fill (0,0,255);
}

else {
fill (0,255,0);
}

}//close draw
```

C.
```
int x = 5;

void setup () {
size (150,150);
}

void draw() {
ellipse (75,75,100,100);

if (x < 4) {
fill (255,0,0);
}
else if (x >= 7) {
fill (100);
}
else if (x < 6) {
fill (0,0,255);
}
else {
fill (0,255,0);
}

}//close draw
```

FIGURE 5.14

LESSON 5.4: LOGICAL OPERATORS DEFINING SPACES

In your projects, you may need to define very specific parameters with your conditional statements. A program may have several animations, boundaries, and/or responsive actions running simultaneously. In order to make sure programming events are all uniquely defined, we often need to conjoin several expressions inside of one condition. To get started on this, run the following program:

```
1  void setup () {
2  size (200,200);
3  }
4
5  void draw() {
6  background (0);
7  rectMode (CENTER);
8  fill (9,215,232);
9  rect (100,100,150,150);
10
11  if (mouseX > 25) {
12  //draw face
13  fill (0);
14  ellipse (70,80,25,25);
15  ellipse (130,80,25,25);
16  fill (255);
17  ellipse (65,75,10,10);
18  ellipse (125,75,10,10);
19  fill (255,0,0);
20  rect (100,140,80,20);
21  }
22
23  }//close draw
24
25
26  //find mouse coordinates
27  void mousePressed() {
28  println ("mouseX=", mouseX, "mouseY", mouseY);
29  }
```

FIGURE 5.15

As you test the program, you will notice that whenever **mouseX** is past 25, the face displays. That is pretty handy but what if we want even more specificity for our rollover face. What about the face displaying whenever our mouse is within *any* side of the blue rectangle? To write a conditional that can specify all of these areas, we will need to use logical operators to conjoin multiple expressions.

Logical Operators

Operator	Expression	Explanation
||	(x>5)||(y<10);	(x is greater than 5) or (y is less than 10)
&&	(x>5)&&(y<10);	(x is greater than 5) and (y is less than 10)
!	!(x);	x is negated (not)

FIGURE 5.16

The logical operator, "or" (expressed with double pipes: | |) conjoins two alternate conditions. If either side of the | | operator is true then the code will be executed. The logical operator "and" (expressed with double ampersands: **&&**) combines conditions. All conditions conjoined by the **&&** operator must be true before the code will be executed. The "not" operator (expressed with an exclamation point:!) is used to negate an expression. We will use this in future chapters. In summary, logical operators combine simple relational statements into more complex expressions.

Returning back to the rollover example from Figure 5.15, we will expand the original **if** statement to cover all 4 sides needed to make a perfectly square rollover. Using the **println()** function inside of **mousePressed()**, we can figure out exactly what coordinates we need to define the boundaries on both the vertical and horizontal axes. Using the **&&** operator, we will rewrite the conditional to cover all four of these sides.

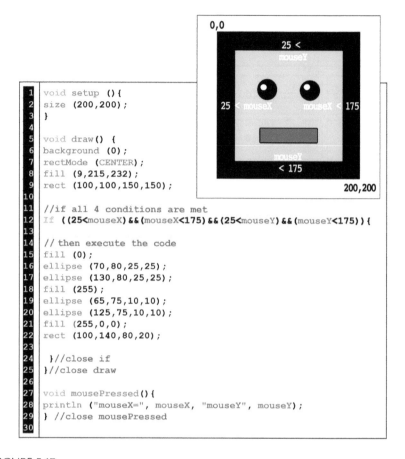

```
1  void setup () {
2  size (200,200);
3  }
4
5  void draw() {
6  background (0);
7  rectMode (CENTER);
8  fill (9,215,232);
9  rect (100,100,150,150);
10
11  //if all 4 conditions are met
12  If ((25<mouseX) && (mouseX<175) && (25<mouseY) && (mouseY<175)) {
13
14  // then execute the code
15  fill (0);
16  ellipse (70,80,25,25);
17  ellipse (130,80,25,25);
18  fill (255);
19  ellipse (65,75,10,10);
20  ellipse (125,75,10,10);
21  fill (255,0,0);
22  rect (100,140,80,20);
23
24  }//close if
25  }//close draw
26
27  void mousePressed() {
28  println ("mouseX=", mouseX, "mouseY", mouseY);
29  } //close mousePressed
30
```

FIGURE 5.17

The previous example illustrates how to define boundaries around all sides of a rectangle using the logical operator, **&&**. It is important to note that parentheses enclose each individual condition and the entire conjoined condition for the sake of clarity. Also, keep an eye out for logical errors when conjoining conditions. In the following example, the condition will never be true because it is logically impossible:

```
1  void draw() {
2
3  //(mouseX is less than 100) && (mouseX is greater than 101)
4  // is not possible!
5  if ((mouseX < 100) && (mouseX > 101)) {
6  ellipse (50,50,50,50); //ellipse will not be drawn.
7  }
8  }
```

FIGURE 5.18

Exercise 5.4

Using the following starter code, figure out the boundaries of the rectangular flashlight. Then write a conditional **if** statement that turns on the yellow light stream only when the mouse hovers over the flashlight.

```
1   void setup () {
2   size (300,300);
3   }
4
5   void draw() {
6   background (0,0,170);
7   fill (255,255,0);
8   triangle (100,0,200,0,150,300);
9   fill (70);
10  rectMode (CENTER);
11  rect (150,250,70,150);
12  fill (100);
13  rect (150,150,70,50);
14  fill (255,0,0);
15  rect (150,170,70,10);
16  }
17
18  void mousePressed() {
19  println("mouseX=",mouseX,"mouseY=",mouseY);
20  }
```

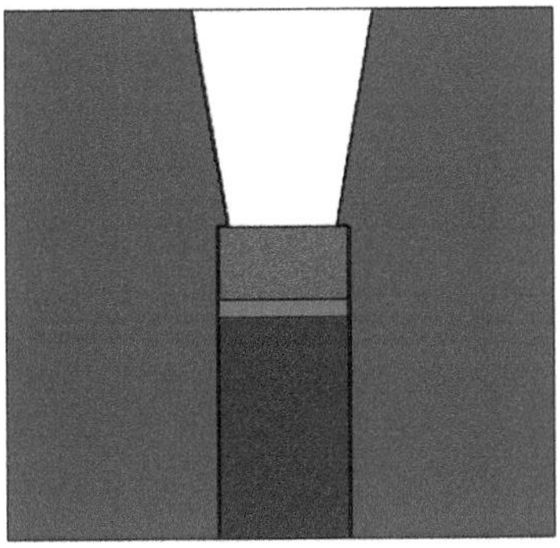

FIGURE 5.19

LESSON 5.5: VARIATIONS WITH MOUSE AND KEYBOARD ACTIONS

The mouse buttons and computer keys offer even more interactive opportunities than previously covered. In Processing, the keyword **mousePressed** has two applications. Inside of **void draw()**, **mousePressed** functions as a *variable* that stores whether or not the mouse button is currently pressed down. But, the **void mousePressed()** *function* (outside of draw) is called only once and then exits after the mouse is pressed down. These principles are similar for **keyPressed()** and **void keyPressed()**. It can be easy to confuse these variations. To see the differences, run the following program and test the actions described in the comments:

```
1   int red1 = 0;
2   int red2 = 0;
3   int green1 = 0;
4   int green2 = 0;
5
6   void setup () {
7     size (200,200);
8   }
9
10  void draw() {
11    background (255);
12
13    //4 ellipses with variable fills
14    fill (red1,0,0);
15    ellipse (50,50,100,100);
16    fill (red2,0,0);
17    ellipse (150,50,100,100);
18    fill (0,green1,0);
19    ellipse (50,150,100,100);
20    fill (0,green2,0);
21    ellipse (150,150,100,100);
22
23    //top left red ellipse
24    if (mousePressed) {
25      red1 = red1 + 1; //hold the mouse down for max red
26    }
27
28    //bottom left green ellipse
29    if (keyPressed) {
30      green1 = green1 + 1; //hold a key down for max green
31    }
32  }
33
34  //top right red ellipse
35  void mousePressed(){
36    red2 = red2 + 1; //click the mouse 255 times for max red
37  }
38
39  //bottom right green ellipse
40  void keyPressed(){
41    green2 = green2 + 1; //click a key 255 times for max green
42  }
```

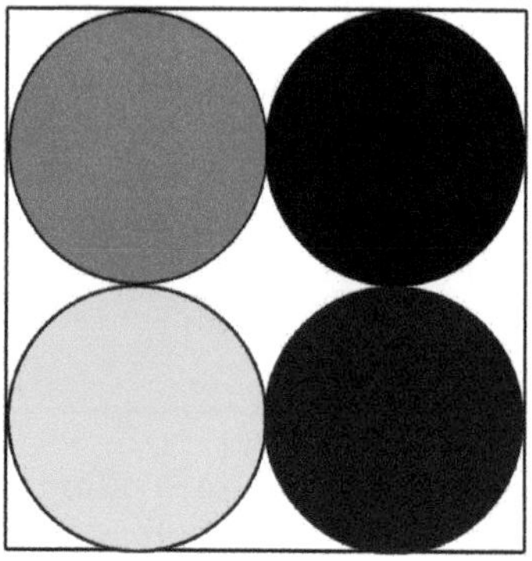

FIGURE 5.20

As you can see, the behaviors for maxing out the colors on each ellipse vary greatly depending on which version of **mousePressed** or **keyPressed** you apply. Also, depending on your machine, the key buttons may behave a bit differently. For certain Operating Systems, holding down a key may cause multiple calls to the function **keyPressed()** while on other machines it will execute only once.

Exercise 5.5

Add onto the following starter program so that:

1. When you hold the mouse down, the black ellipse goes left while the red ellipse goes right.

2. When you hold a key down, the green ellipse moves up while the blue ellipse moves down.

```
1  int moveL = 100;
2  int moveR = 100;
3  int moveUp = 100;
4  int moveDown = 100;
5
6  void setup () {
7  size (200,200);
8  }
9
10 void draw() {
11 background (255);
12
13 //black
14 fill (0);
15 ellipse (moveL,100,80,80);
16
17 //red
18 fill (255,0,0);
19 ellipse (moveR,100,60,60);
20
21 //green
22 fill (0,255,0);
23 ellipse (100,moveUp,40,40);
24
25 //blue
26 fill (0,0,255);
27 ellipse (100,moveDown,20,20);
28 }
```

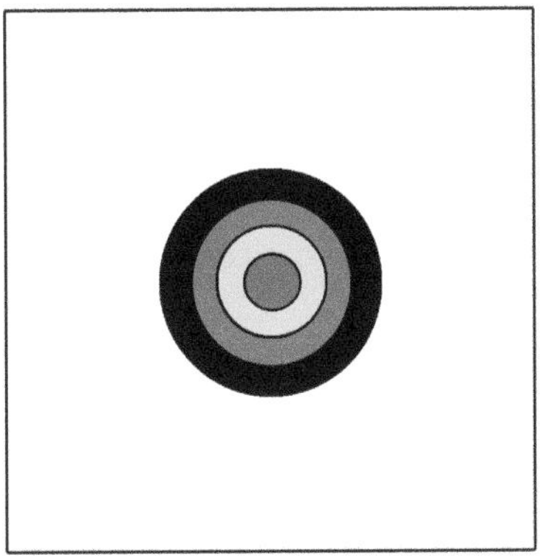

FIGURE 5.21

LESSON 5.6: TWO VARIABLES: ALTERNATING MOVEMENTS

Now, we will program a traveling shape to change its direction when crossing a boundary. In order to do this, we need to use *two* custom variables: one for the shape's position and the other for its directional velocity. Typically, when we move a shape to the right, we add to the position variable and when we move to the left, we subtract.

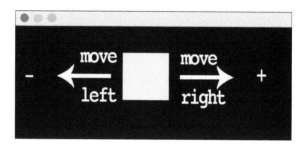

FIGURE 5.22

But, to make a shape switch between two directions, we need to alternate between positive *and* negative values. To do this, we will add to our program a velocity variable, multiply it by −1, and capitalize on the following mathematical concepts:

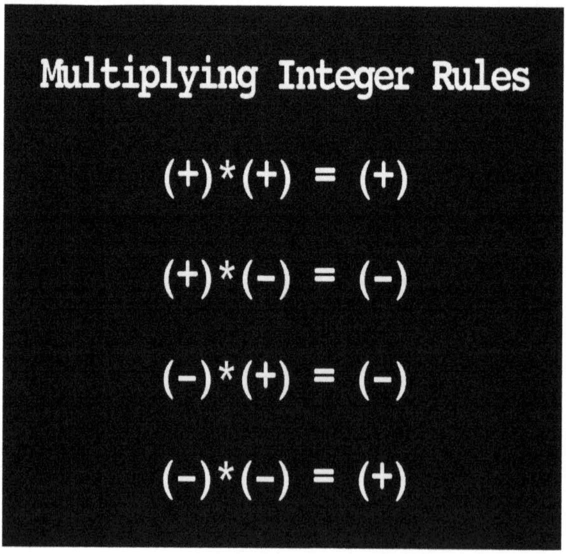

Multiplying Integer Rules

$$(+)*(+) = (+)$$

$$(+)*(-) = (-)$$

$$(-)*(+) = (-)$$

$$(-)*(-) = (+)$$

FIGURE 5.23

Using these principles, we will alternate a variable between positive and negative. To see how this works, run the following program:

```
1   int x = 100;   //starting position
2   int velx = 1;//velocity
3
4   void setup() {
5   size(200,200);
6   }
7
8   void draw() {
9   background(0);
10  rectMode (CENTER);
11  fill(255,255,0);
12
13  rect(x,100,50,50);
14  x = x + velx;
15
16  if ((x<0)||(x>200)){ //if x gets to either side of canvas,
17  velx = velx * -1;   //then change the direction of velx
18  }
19
20  //variable reports shows directional change
21  println ("x=",x);
22  println ("velx=",velx);
23  }//close draw
```

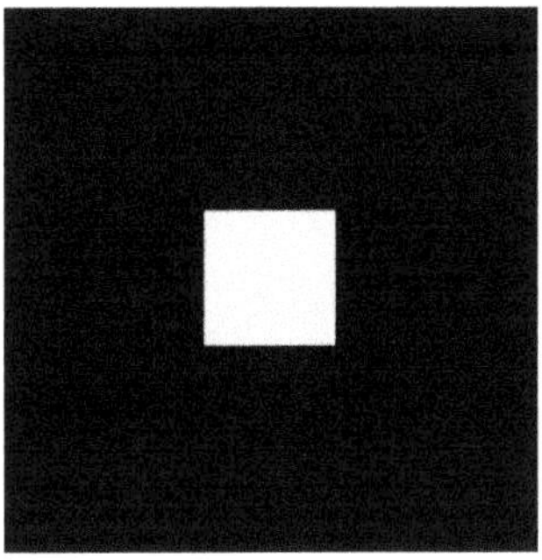

FIGURE 5.24

In the above example, we use the "or" logical operator (| |) to create a choice of two conditions. If the position variable "x" becomes less than 0 *or* greater than 200 then "velx" is multiplied by –1. Due to the principles of multiplying integers (Figure 5.23), "velx" alternates between positive and negative values each time it crosses one of these boundaries. Thus, the assignment operator that causes the square's movement (x = x + velx) updates and alternates the direction of the traveling square.

Exercise 5.6

For the following exercise, download the folder: "Chapter 5 Lesson Imagery" from the publisher's website. Then, run the starter code with the image file "planet.png" inside of the data folder (see Lesson 4.1 for more information on loading images).

```
1  int y = 150;
2  int vely = 4;
3  PImage planet;
4
5  void setup() {
6  size(300,300);
7  planet = loadImage("planet.png");
8  noSmooth();
9  }
10
11 void draw() {
12 background(0);
13 imageMode (CENTER);
14 fill(255,0,255);
15 image(planet,150,y);
16 }
```

FIGURE 5.25

a. Program the planet to bounce up and down.

b. Now, implement a second variable with a different velocity so that the planet bounces off all 4 walls.

LESSON 5.7: COLOR DETECTION USING THE GET() FUNCTION

So far, animation boundaries have been programmed cleanly in rectangular regions. But, at some point you may need to activate a rounded or odd shaped region in your project. You can do this using color detection with the **get()** function. There are 16,777,216 possible RGB colors and Processing's **get()** function can detect them all. The 3 values (R,G,B) that we are used to seeing in color commands like **fill()** and **stroke()** can be replaced by number codes provided by the **get()** function. To see color detection in action with the **get()** function, run the following program:

```
int c; //variable for storing color values

void setup () {
size (200,200);
}

void draw() {
background (0);
stroke (255);
strokeWeight (5);

//green
fill (22,118,54); //same as (-15305162)
ellipse (100,100,150,150);

//fuschia
fill (-2942327); //same as (211,26,137);
ellipse (100,100,100,100);

//blue
fill (-14916733); //same as (28,99,131);
ellipse (100,100,50,50);

//"c" gets the color of 1 pixel wherever the mouse is
c = get (mouseX,mouseY);
}

//print the color value of "c"
void mousePressed(){
println (c);
}
```

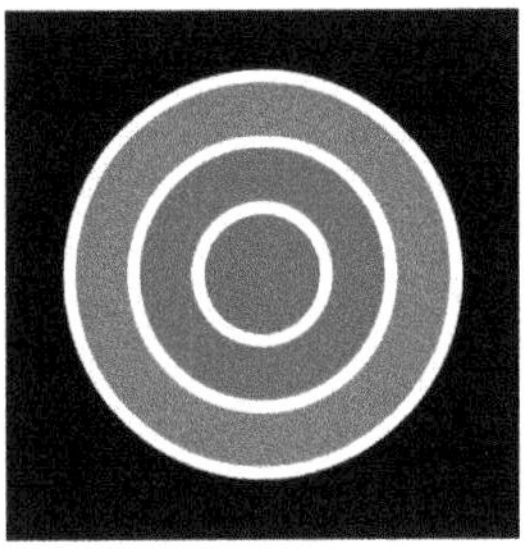

FIGURE 5.26

If you click on each color and observe the **println()** report, you will see that **get()** grabs a color value from wherever the mouse is. The color values are then assigned to a variable named "c." Now, "c" is available for further programming (which we will see in the next example). Before moving forward, it is important to note that where you place the **get()** command matters. The **get()** function can only detect the colors of shapes and images that are placed *before* it in a program. You can test this for yourself by moving **get()** up higher in the program.

Now, we will implement the **get()** command to create a rollover face responsive to color detection. Run the following program:

```
1   int c; //variable to hold color values
2
3   void setup () {
4   size (200,200);
5   }
6
7   void draw() {
8   background (0);
9   rectMode (CENTER);
10  fill (9,215,232); //same color value as -16132120
11  ellipse (100,100,150,150);
12
13  //use the mouse to find colors and store them in "c";
14  c = get (mouseX,mouseY);
15
16  //if "c" matches the color of the big blue ellipse
17  if (c == -16132120){
18
19  //then draw face
20  fill (0);
21  ellipse (70,80,25,25);
22  ellipse (130,80,25,25);
23  fill (255);
24  ellipse (65,75,10,10);
25  ellipse (125,75,10,10);
26  fill (255,0,0);
27  rect (100,140,80,20);
28   }//close if
29  }//close draw
30
31  //color detection report
32  void mousePressed(){
33  println (c);
34  }
```

FIGURE 5.27

As you can see, this strategy provides a nice alternative for creating active regions in your projects. However, this technique is specific to solid color detection and will be less reliable with multicolored images and photos. Also, don't forget to keep in mind that the order of your code matters when placing the **get()** command. Always, put **get()** just after the shapes, you need color detection on. If you put **get()** after shape functions that you don't need color detection information on, then you may see your animations glitch. In the previous example, you can see this glitching in action by moving **get()** down in the program just before the close of **void draw()**.

When you hover over an eye, the animation flickers because **get()** is dealing with two color layers, one causing the **if** conditional to fulfill and the other causing it to exit.

Exercise 5.7

For the following exercise, download the folder: "Chapter 5 Lesson Imagery" from the publisher's website. Next, run the following starter code with the image file "balloons.png" inside of the data folder (see Lesson 4.1 for more info on loading images).

```
1  //image
2  PImage balloons;
3
4  //color detector variable
5  int c;
6
7  //movement variable
8  int move = 250;
9
10 void setup (){
11 size (400,400);
12 balloons = loadImage("balloons.png");
13 }
14
15 void draw() {
16 background (144,207,240);
17 imageMode (CENTER);
18 image(balloons, 200, move);
19
20 //button
21 fill (0); //same as -16777216
22 ellipse (20,20,20,20);
23
24 //get a color and store in 'c'
25 c = get (mouseX,mouseY);
26
27 //if 'c' is black then move balloons up
28 if (c == -16777216){
29 move = move - 1;
30   }
31
32 }///close draw
33
34 //color detection report
35 void mousePressed(){
36 println ("c=",c);
37 }
```

FIGURE 5.28

In the previous starter code, the balloons move up when you hover your mouse over the small, black ellipse. Now, program the following additions:

a. Place a white **ellipse()** of the same size underneath the black **ellipse()**.

b. Find the numerical color code for white.

c. Add an **else if** conditional statement that makes the balloons move down when you hover your mouse over the white **ellipse()**.

PROJECT: ROLLOVER ANIMATION

Create a responsive animation that transforms when the mouse hovers over different parts of the canvas. Consider selecting shapes/images that work together to create several animation frames of one subject. Think of this project as bringing to life an object, space, or creature. See project examples in the downloads folder available from the publisher's website.

FIGURE 5.29 Student project example: rollover animation. (Printed with permission from Amelia Berry.)

FIGURE 5.30 Student project example: rollover animation. (Printed with permission from Connor Port.)

FIGURE 5.31   Project example of animated bear.

CHAPTER 6

Events and Interactions for Simple Games: Part 1

FIGURE 6.1   Student project example: scrolling video game. (Printed with permission from Elijah Devillanueva.)

In Chapters 6 and 7, the concepts presented are meant to be used as parts for a more complex project such as a multilevel game or interactive narrative. Because these examples fit into larger architectures presented in

Chapter 8, the final master project will be tackled at the end of this book. Use these next three chapters to test ideas as you plan for your concluding project.

It is also important to note that programs constructed from these examples can be arranged in a variety of ways depending on the creator's vision. As you move through these chapters and later develop a more complex project on your own, there will be new challenges. This is because each producer's goals are different and there is no exact template for an original project.

One of the most important aspects of creating a successful outcome is a clear understanding of the *conditional logic* structures in your project. Your computer will execute your vision based on the structures you design. Sometimes there are unintended results when programming a series of events with multiple conditions and outcomes. Often, a slight adjustment of brackets will make all the difference in the functionality of your project. Fitting the different pieces together will take some practice. However, with plenty of experimentation (and a personal archive of annotated code examples), your work will eventually click!

FIGURE 6.2   Student project example: scrolling video game. (Printed with permission from Elijah Devillanueva.)

LESSON 6.1: TURNING THINGS ON WITH BOOLEAN VARIABLES

Thus far, we have exclusively used the numerical variable types: floats and integers. These variables usually count up or down and animate designs/ events over time. However, sometimes we might need a simple switch that turns an event on or off. For these purposes, we will use boolean variables (named after the mathematician, George Boole). Booleans are assigned a value of **true** or **false** and nothing else.

TABLE 6.1 Commonly Used Variables

Type	Naming Conventions	Values	Declared and Initialized Examples
Integer	Most any word (without spaces) except for keywords that are built into Processing.	whole numbers	int move = −5; int jump = 3;
Float	"	decimal numbers	float fly = 5.0; float change = −0.5;
Boolean	"	**true** or **false**	boolean button = **true**; boolean switch = **false**;

Run the following example:

```
1  boolean button = false; //"button" starts as false
2
3  void setup () {
4  size (200,200);
5  }
6
7  void draw (){
8  background (239,71,255);
9  noStroke();
10
11 if (button == true) {  //if "button" is true
12 fill (255,76,31);      //then the fill is red
13 }
14
15 else {         //otherwise
16 fill (255);  //the fill is white
17 }
18
19 ellipse (width/2, height/2,150,150);
20 } //close draw
21
22 void mousePressed(){ //mouse pressed
23 button = true;       //makes the "button" true
24 }
```

FIGURE 6.3

In Figure 6.3, there are two conditions the computer must check for. If the boolean variable, "button" returns as **true**, then we will see a red fill. Otherwise, if the "button" variable returns as **false**, then the **else** statement will trigger a white fill. And, since "button" is initialized as **false**, the **ellipse()** starts out white. But, when the mouse is pressed, "button" becomes **true** and the **fill()** becomes red.

Exercise 6.1

Create a black canvas that is 200 × 200 pixels. Write a program that uses a conditional statement with a boolean variable that starts with a red **ellipse()** and changes to blue **rect()** when the mouse is pressed.

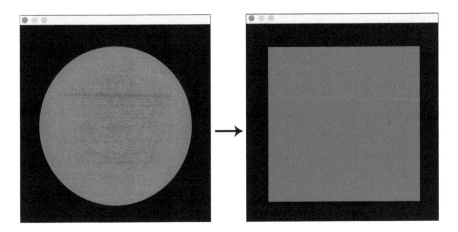

FIGURE 6.4

LESSON 6.2: TOGGLING BETWEEN TWO STATES USING BOOLEAN VARIABLES

As introduced in Chapter 5, the use of relational and logical operators (Figure 6.5) is key to programming complex interactions. In the previous example, we used a boolean variable to turn something on. Now, we will implement the negation operator (!) to create a switch that alternates between on and off.

Relational Operators

Operator	Expression	Explanation
<	X < Y	X is less than Y
< =	X <= Y	X is less than or equal to Y
>	X > Y	X is greater than Y
> =	X >= Y	X is greater than or equal to Y
= =	X == Y	X is equivalent to Y
!=	X! = Y	X is not equivalent to Y

Logical Operators

Operator	Expression	Explanation
||	(x>5)||(y<10);	(x is greater than 5) or (y is less than 10)
&&	(x>5)&&(y<10);	(x is greater than 5) and (y is less than 10)
!	!(x);	x is negated (not)

FIGURE 6.5

In order to create the alternating states of "on" and "off", we will program a boolean variable to *negate* itself (variable =! variable). Since a boolean variable can only be **true** or **false**, every time a certain condition is fulfilled, the boolean variable will switch to its opposite value. Run the following program:

```
1  boolean circle1 = false;
2
3  void setup () {
4  size (450,150);
5  }
6
7  void draw (){
8  background (255);
9  fill (0);
10
11 if (circle1) { //if circle1 becomes true
12 ellipse (75,75,150,150); //then draw an ellipse
13 }
14
15 println ("circle1=",circle1); //variable report
16
17 }//close draw
18
19 void mousePressed () {
20
21 //if the mouse is pressed on the left side
22 if ((mouseX > 0) && (mouseX < 150)){
23
24 //then negate the value of the circle1 variable
25 circle1 = !circle1;
26   }
27
28 } //close mousePressed
```

FIGURE 6.6

Whenever the mouse is clicked on the left side of the screen, the boolean variable "circle1" alternates between **true** and **false**. If "circle1" is **true**, then the black ellipse is drawn. If the "circle1" returns **false**, then the black ellipse is not drawn. Also, it is important to note that we see a new shorthand for writing a boolean variable as **true**:

if (circle1) is the same as **if (circle1 == true)**.

Exercise 6.2

Add onto the previous example (Figure 6.6), by programming two more black ellipses as button switches. Program these two new ellipses so that they also toggle on and off when clicked in their respective regions.

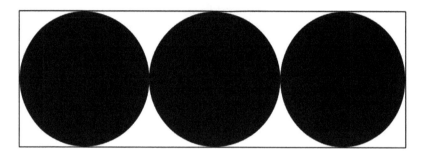

FIGURE 6.7

LESSON 6.3: MULTIPLE BUTTONS ALTERNATING

In the previous exercise, all of the black ellipses can be turned on, or off, or in combinations of on and off. But, what if you want each button to be limited so that only one can be turned on at a time. There are different ways to explore this but the next example shows a direct and consistent solution. Run the following program:

```
1  boolean button1 = false;
2  boolean button2 = false;
3
4  void setup () {
5  size (200,600);
6  }
7
8  void draw (){
9  background (0);
10 stroke (255);
11 line (0,200,200,200);
12 line (0,400,200,400);
13
14 if (button1) { //if button1 is true, draw a red ellipse
15 fill (255,0,0);
16 ellipse (100,100,150,150);
17 }
18
19 if (button2) { // if button2 is true, draw a yellow ellipse
20 fill (255,255,0);
21 ellipse (100, 300,150,150);
22 }
23
24 //variable report
25 println ("button1",button1);
26 println ("button2",button2);
27
28 }//close draw
29
30 void mousePressed () {
31
32 //if the top section is clicked only button1 can be true
33 if ((mouseY > 0) && (mouseY < 200)){
34 button1 = true;
35 button2 = false;
36 }
37
38 //if the middle section is clicked only button2 can be true
39 if ((mouseY > 200)&&(mouseY < 400)){
40 button1 = false;
41 button2 = true;
42 }
43 } //close mousePressed
```

FIGURE 6.8

In the previous example, the canvas is sectioned into 3 regions (upper, middle, and bottom). The top two regions can only have one boolean variable be **true** at a time. This is because we have specified that if one boolean becomes **true** (in a particular region), then the other boolean becomes **false**. So, if the top red light is on, then the yellow light is off and vice versa.

Exercise 6.3

Complete the previous example (Figure 6.8) with a third green **ellipse()** button on the bottom. Program the three sections so that only one color can be turned on at a time.

FIGURE 6.9

LESSON 6.4: BOOLEANS WORKING WITH NUMERICAL VARIABLES

Together, booleans and numerical variables offer endless possibilities for time-based events, animations, and action triggers. Run the following program:

```
1  float x = 25;
2  boolean going = false;
3
4  void setup () {
5  size (300,150);
6  }
7
8  void draw () {
9  background (255,79,103);
10 rectMode (CENTER);
11 fill (189,192,255);
12 rect (x, 75, 50, 50);
13
14 if (going) { //while "going" is true
15 x = x + 2;   //the assignment operator will increase x
16 }
17
18 }//close draw
19
20 void mousePressed (){ //every time the mouse is pressed,
21 going = !going; //toggle "going" between true and false
22 }
```

FIGURE 6.10

Although this example is simple, it demonstrates a helpful structure for triggering animation actions on demand. The assignment operator only increases by 2 when "going" is **true**. As long as "going" remains **true**, the rectangle will move right. If the mouse is pressed again, "going" becomes **false** and the assignment operator is no longer active.

Exercise 6.4

Type the following starter code:

```
1   boolean shoot = false;
2   int y = 150;
3
4   void setup () {
5   size (150,300);
6   }
7
8   void draw () {
9   rectMode (CENTER);
10  background (0,0,150);
11
12  //canon ball (red ellipse)
13  fill (255,0,0);
14  ellipse (75,y,50,50);
15
16  //canon
17  fill (100);
18  rect (75,250,50,200);
19  fill (50);
20  rect (75,150,50,20);
21
22  }//close draw
23
24  void mousePressed(){
25  shoot = true;
26  }
```

FIGURE 6.11

a. Now, add a conditional **if** statement into **void draw()** that causes the red ellipse to travel upward when the mouse is pressed.

b. Next, inside of **void mousePressed()**, add another **if** statement that resets the variable "y" to 150 when it is less than 0.

LESSON 6.5: SPECIFIC KEYBOARD INTERACTIONS

The keyboard also offers a world of possibilities for programming interactivity. Run the following program:

```
1  float redx = 0;
2  float bluex = 400;
3  boolean redgoing = false;
4  boolean bluegoing = false;
5
6  void setup(){
7  size (400,200);
8  }
9
10 void draw(){
11 background (255,249,105);
12
13 //red ellipse
14 fill (255,79,103);
15 ellipse (redx, 50, 100,100);
16 if (redgoing){
17 redx = redx + 2;
18 }
19
20 //blue ellipse
21 fill (54,191,255);
22 ellipse (bluex,150, 100,100);
23 if (bluegoing){
24 bluex = bluex - 3;
25   }
26
27 }//close draw
28
29 void keyPressed(){ //if a key is pressed
30
31 if (key == '1'){ //and if the key is 1
32 redgoing = !redgoing; //change the state of "redgoing"
33   }
34
35 if (key == '9'){ //and if the key is 9
36 bluegoing = !bluegoing; //change the state of "bluegoing"
37   }
38
39 }//close keypressed
```

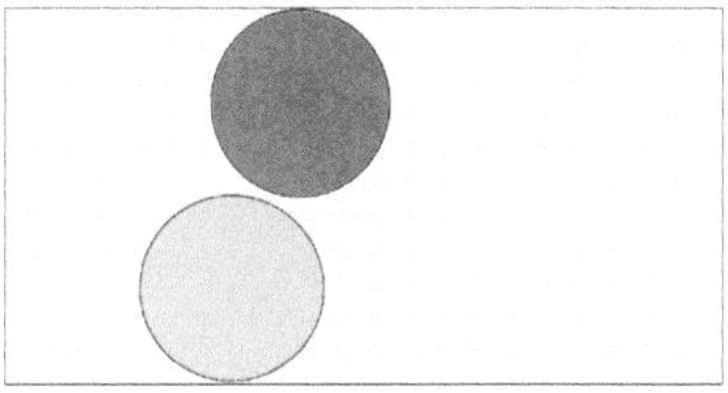

FIGURE 6.12

The previous example shows the beginning idea of a two player game using the number keys "1" and "9". As with the two versions of **mousePressed**, there are two versions of **keyPressed** in Processing but **keyPressed** offers even more possibilities due to the many keys available. The following table explains the syntax for commonly used keys and functions.

TABLE 6.2   Keyboard Programming Syntax

	keyPressed	*void keyPressed( )*
Description	A built-in variable typically used inside of **void draw( )** that is activated by holding a key down.	An independent function outside of **void draw( )** that is called once every time a key is pressed.
Example without a specified key	```void draw () {
if (keyPressed) {
//code to execute
}
}```	```void keyPressed(){
//code to execute
}```
Example using a specified number key	```void draw() {
  if (keyPressed){

    if (key == '1') {
    //code to execute
    }

  } //close keyPressed
} //close draw``` | ```void keyPressed(){

  if (key == '1'){
  //code to execute
  }

} //close keyPressed()``` |
| Example using a specified letter key | ```void draw(){

if (keypressed){
  if (key == 'a' || key == 'A'){
  //code to execute
  }

} //close keyPressed()
}   //close draw``` | ```void keyPressed(){

  if (key == 'a' || key == 'A'){
  //code to execute
  }

} //close keyPressed()``` |
| Example using arrow keys | ```void draw() {
  if (keyPressed){

  if (keyCode == RIGHT){
  //code to execute
  }
    else if (keyCode == LEFT) {
  //code to execute
  }
    else if (keyCode == UP) {
  //code to execute
  }
    else if (keyCode == DOWN) {
  //code to execute
  }

  } //close keyPressed
}//close draw``` | ```void keyPressed(){

  if (keyCode == RIGHT) {
  //code to execute;
  }
  else if (keyCode == LEFT){
  //code to execute;
  }
  else if (keyCode == UP) {
  //code to execute;
  }
  else if (keyCode == DOWN) {
  //code to execute;
  }

} //close keyPressed()``` |

(See the Processing reference for key codes not presented in this table.)

Exercise 6.5

For the following exercise, download the folder: "Chapter 6 Lesson Imagery" from the publisher's website. Next, run the following starter code with the image file "face.png" inside of the data folder (see Lesson 4.1 for more info on loading images).

```
1  PImage face;
2  int x = 150;
3  int y = 150;
4
5  void setup(){
6  size( 300, 300 );
7  face = loadImage ("face.png");
8  }
9
10  void draw(){
11  background(0);
12  imageMode (CENTER);
13  image (face,x, y);
14  } //close draw
15
16
17  void keyPressed(){
18
19    if (keyCode == RIGHT) {
20    x = x + 5;
21    }
22
23    else if (keyCode == LEFT) {
24    x = x - 5;
25    }
26
27  }//close keyPressed
```

FIGURE 6.13

Now, finish the code so that the face also moves up and down with the corresponding arrow keys.

LESSON 6.6: CREATING A WALKING CHARACTER

FIGURE 6.14   Student project example: walking character. (Printed with permission from Angelica Quevedo.)

Now, we will combine keyboard interactivity with the toggle of a boolean variable to simulate a walking character composed from two 8-bit styled, animation frames. From the download folder, "Chapter 6 Lesson

Imagery" import the images "friend1.png" and "friend2.png" inside of a data folder and run the following program:

```
1  PImage position1;
2  PImage position2;
3
4  int x = 200; //character movement variable
5  boolean walk = false; //picture changing variable
6
7  void setup (){
8  size (400,200);
9  position1 = loadImage("friend1.png");
10 position2 = loadImage ("friend2.png");
11 }
12
13 void draw (){
14 noStroke();
15 background (14,201,184);
16 fill (90,131,77);
17 rect (0,150,400,50);
18
19 if (walk==false){
20 image(position1,x,60); //load position 1 image
21 }
22
23 else if (walk==true){
24 image(position2,x,60); //load position 2 image
25 }
26
27 }//close draw
28
29 void keyPressed(){
30 walk = !walk; //alternate "walk" between true and false
31
32 if (keyCode==LEFT){ //if the left arrow key is pressed
34 x=x-10; //then move images left
35 }
36
37 if (keyCode==RIGHT){ //if the right arrow key pressed
38 x=x+10; //then move images right
39 }
40
41 } //close keyPressed
```

FIGURE 6.15

In the previous example, one x-position variable controls the placement of two different images. These two images alternately load every time a key is pressed and thus create the appearance of a walking animation. The direction of the animation is controlled by the left and right arrow keys.

Exercise 6.6

Write a program using the images "rocketa.png" and "rocketb.png" (from the "Chapter 6 Lesson Imagery" download folder), that alternates between the two rocket images and moves up/down with the corresponding arrow keys.

FIGURE 6.16

LESSON 6.7: BOUNDARIES

Now that we have the tools to create more complex keyboard controls, we may want to limit where users can move to on the canvas. Depending on the goals of your specific project, you might have placed a fence in your design to tell a story or positioned a net to create a game. Boundaries, (sometimes called "hitboxes") are very useful for illustrated, interactive works. To see a boundary structure in action, run the following program:

```
1  int rectx = 200; //x position of green rect
2  int recty = 100; //y position of green rect
3
4  void setup(){
5  size (400,200);
6  }
7
8  void draw() {
9  background(224,211,173);
10 noStroke();
11 rectMode (CENTER);
12
13 //green square controlled by arrow keys
14 fill (53,148,119);
15 rect(rectx, recty, 50, 50);
16
17 //purple rectangles
18 fill (128,10,148);
19 rect(200,25,400,50);
20 rect(200,175,400,50);
21 rect(25,100,50,200);
22 rect(375,100,50,200);
23
24 //boundaries
25 if (rectx < 72){ //left side
26 rectx = 72;
27 }
28 else if (rectx > 324){ //right side
29 rectx = 324;
30 }
31
32 //variable report to find hitbox boundaries
34 println ("rectx=",rectx,"recty=",recty);
35 } //close draw
36
37 void keyPressed() {
38 if (keyCode == LEFT) {
39 rectx -= 6; //shorthand syntax, same as: rectx = rectx - 6;
40 }
41 else if (keyCode == RIGHT) {
42 rectx += 6; //shorthand syntax, same as: rectx = rectx + 6;
43 }
44 } //close keyPressed
```

FIGURE 6.17

In Figure 6.17, the arrow keys are programmed to control the horizontal movement of the green **rect()**. But, when the green **rect()** touches the left or right side of the purple boundaries – it bounces back. This is because there is a conditional statement resetting the variable "rectx" on both sides. If, when moving to the left, variable "rectx" becomes smaller than 72, then "rectx" is reset back to 72. On the right side, if "rectx" becomes larger than 324, then it is reset back to 324. To easily determine these boundary values, we can watch the **println()** report in the black console window while moving the green square to a boundary position. Also, it is important to note that there is a new shorthand for writing assignment operators. Figure 6.18 summarizes this shortcut syntax:

```
      SHORTHAND  FOR  COMMON
      ASSIGNMENT  OPERATORS

If adding or subtracting 1 from a variable:
    x = x + 1; is equivalent to x++;
    x = x - 1; is equivalent to x--;


    To simplify other math operations:
    x = x + 2; is equivalent to x+=2;
    x = x - 3; is equivalent to x-=3;
    x = x * 4; is equivalent to x*=4;
    x = x / 5; is equivalent to x/=5;
```

FIGURE 6.18

Exercise 6.7

Modify the code example from Figure 6.17 with the following additions:

a. Program the green square to move up and down with the corresponding arrow keys.

b. Program top and bottom purple boundaries.

This concludes, Chapter 6: Events and Interactions for Simple Games: Part 1. Displayed in this chapter (as well as the next two), are screenshots from student projects utilizing all lessons from this book. The download folder at the end of Chapter 8 contains program examples of all of the student projects pictured plus more. Feel free to look ahead at these examples, but please note that these projects contain lessons not covered yet and it is recommended that you complete Chapters 7 and 8 before starting your final project.

FIGURE 6.19 Student project example: three level, puzzle game. (Printed with permission from Gillian Probert.)

CHAPTER 7

Events and Interactions for Simple Games: Part 2

FIGURE 7.1   Student project example: interactive, memory game. (Printed with permission from Lorena Bustillos.)

In this chapter, we will explore another set of commonly used procedures for making games and multilayered projects. We will start by programming timers. Clocked events are frequently used for triggering game interactions and user outcomes. Next, we will dig into the efficiency of **for** loops by generating number sets and multiple shape iterations. Along the way, we will also explore a keyboard control system that implements continuous motion and a two-player jumping game. Also prominent in this chapter is an overview of two strategies for programming collision detections. For our purposes, collisions occur when two images/shapes intersect on the canvas. For example, an animated character colliding with a moving obstacle or a reward graphic. Think of Mrs. Pacman, colliding with the blue ghosts (obstacles) or eating the jumping fruits (rewards). By implementing detectable collisions, projects can be enhanced with scoreboards, scenery changes, accelerated levels, or whatever your imagination dictates. As with Chapter 6, the examples here are pieces meant to fit into a larger project of your designing. An unpacking of multilevel project architectures will be presented in Chapter 8.

FIGURE 7.2   Student project example: play characters from a matching memory game. (Printed with permission from Lorena Bustillos.)

LESSON 7.1: TIMERS

There is nothing more exciting than a countdown. Countdowns place pressure on users working through a timed event such as a video game hunt or race. There are several ways to program a timer but in this lesson, we will create a seconds timer by manipulating Processing's built-in variable, **frameCount**. In Processing, **frameCount** holds the number of frames that have been displayed after a program starts. By default, Processing loads 60 frames per second and this value offers an opportunity to easily track when a second has passed. To execute this opportunity, we will implement the "modulo operator," which is represented in Processing by the percentage symbol: %. Modulo reports, the remainder of two numbers divided. For example, 20 divided by 3 is 6, *with a remainder of 2*. So, 20% 3 = 2.

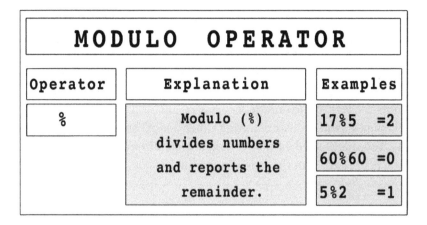

FIGURE 7.3

Run the following program to see how modulo (%) and **frameCount** work together to create a timer:

```
1   int timer = 9; //countdown starts at 9
2
3   void setup() {
4   size(200, 200);
5   }
6
7   void draw() {
8   //display "timer" variable
9   background(0,0,255);
10  fill (255);
11  textAlign(CENTER,CENTER);
12  textSize(100);
13  text(timer, width/2, height/2);
14
15  if (frameCount % 60 == 0) { //if a second has passed
16  timer = timer - 1;//subtract 1 from the timer countdown.
17  }
18  }
```

FIGURE 7.4

Here, the modulo operator is used to determine if an exact second has passed. Remember, that by default the **void draw()** cycle runs at 60 frames per second. So, when the **frameCount** is divided by 60, modulo (%) returns a remainder of 0. Thus, every time modulo (%) returns 0 – a second has passed. We plug this calculation into a conditional **if** statement, which subtracts 1 one from the "timer" variable each time the second mark is hit. The "timer" variable is also displayed as a countdown on the canvas window with the **text()** command (see Chapter 2). Whereas, before we used **text()** to print words, now we use it to print the fluctuating value of a variable (no quotes needed). Also, note the usage of **textAlign()**, which anchors the text in the middle.

Perhaps a continuously counting timer doesn't suit your programming goals. You might need a timer to stop at a certain number or reset when a button is pressed. Run the following example:

```
1  int timer = 5; //countdown starts at 5
2  boolean stop = false; //timer stop switch
3
4  void setup() {
5  size(200, 200);
6  }
7
8  void draw() {
9  //timer display
10 background(255,100,255);
11 textSize(150);
12 fill (255);
13 textAlign(CENTER,CENTER);
14 text(timer, 100,100);
15
16 if (frameCount % 60 == 0){ //if a second passes,
17 timer = timer - 1; //then subtract 1 from the "timer"
18 }
19
20 if (timer==0){ //if the "timer" gets to 0,
21 stop = true;   //then turn "stop" to true
22 }
23
24 if (stop==true){//if "stop" is true,
25 timer = 0; //then keep "timer" at 0
26 }
27
28 if (keyPressed){ //if a key is pressed
29 stop = false; //then restart the timer at 5
30 timer = 5;
31  }
32 }//close draw
```

FIGURE 7.5

In the previous example (Figure 7.5), we've implemented a countdown with a boolean variable called "stop" inside of **void draw()**. When the "timer" variable counts down to 0, "stop" becomes **true** holding the "timer" variable at 0. To create a reset button, we use **void keyPressed()** to reset and restart the countdown whenever a key is pressed.

Exercise 7.1

Program a timer displayed on a green canvas that counts *up* from 0 to 5, and resets/restarts whenever the *mouse* is pressed.

FIGURE 7.6

LESSON 7.2: CONTINUOUS MOTION KEY CONTROLS

In Chapter 6, we looked at strategies for keyboard controls that moved shapes incrementally with each key press. Now, we will tackle another popular keyboard control style often used in video games: multidirectional, continuous motion. Run the following example:

```
//position of ellipse
float x=20;
float y=20;

//speed of ellipse motion
float speed= 2.5;

//direction controls
int directionX = 0;
int directionY = 0;

void setup(){
size(300, 300);
}

void draw(){
background(255,55,76);
stroke(255);
fill (202,12,232);
ellipse (x, y, 50, 50);

//continuous directional motion controlled by keys
x = x + (speed * directionX);
y = y + (speed * directionY);

} //close draw

void keyPressed() {

if (keyCode == LEFT){
 directionX= -1; //x's movement is left
 directionY= 0;  //y's movement is stopped
}
else if (keyCode == RIGHT){
 directionX= 1;  //x's movement is right
 directionY= 0;  //y's movement is stopped
}

//code continued in next figure
```

FIGURE 7.7 (Code example continued in Figure 7.8).

```
40  else if (keyCode == UP){
41   directionX= 0;  //x's movement is stopped
42   directionY= -1; //y's movement is up
43  }
44
45  else if (keyCode == DOWN){
46   directionX = 0; //x's movement is stopped
47   directionY= 1;  //y's movement is down
48  }
49
50  else if (keyCode == SHIFT) {
51   directionX= 0;  //x's movement is stopped
52   directionY= 0;  //y's movement is stopped
53   }
54
55  }//close keyPressed
```

FIGURE 7.8

In the previous example (Figures 7.7–7.8), it is the placement of the assignment operators (code lines 23, 24) *inside* of **void draw()** that facilitate the continuous motion of the **ellipse()**. Triggered by the arrow keys, the movements change direction depending on what values are assigned to "directionX" and "directionY". The following table presents this example in detail.

TABLE 7.1   Notes on Directional Keyboard Motion (Figures 7.7–7.8).

Key Pressed	Variable Values	Assignment Operation $x = x + (speed * directionX)$; $y = y + (speed * directionY)$;	Outcome
Left	directionX = −1; directionY = 0;	$x = x + (2.5 * -1)$; $y = y + (2.5 * 0)$;	$x = x - 2.5$; //move left $y = y + 0$; //no y axis travel
Right	directionX = 1; directionY = 0;	$x = x + (2.5 * 1)$; $y = y + (2.5 * 0)$;	$x = x + 2.5$; //move right $y = y + 0$; //no y axis travel
Up	directionX = 0; directionY = −1;	$x = x + (2.5 * 0)$; $y = y + (2.5 * -1)$;	$x = x + 0$; //no x axis travel $y = y - 2.5$; //move up
Down	directionX = 0; directionY = 1;	$x = x + (2.5 * 0)$; $y = y + (2.5 * 1)$;	$x = x + 0$; //no x axis travel $y = y + 2.5$; //move down
Shift	directionX = 0; directionY = 0;	$x = x + (2.5 * 0)$; $y = y + (2.5 * 0)$;	$x = x + 0$; //no x axis travel $y = y + 0$; //no y axis travel

Exercise 7.2

Building onto the previous example (Figures 7.7–7.8), program boundaries for all 4 sides of the canvas so that the ellipse is unable to move off screen. (For a review on creating boundaries, see Lesson 6.7.)

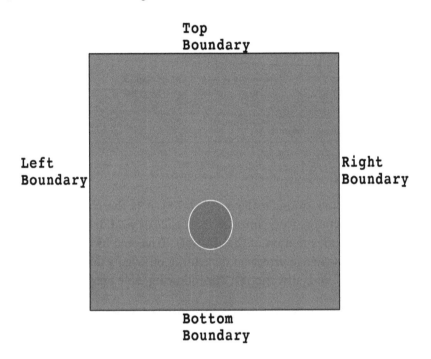

FIGURE 7.9

LESSON 7.3: FOR LOOPS ARE EFFICIENT

What, if your project required 100 shapes to be displayed simultaneously on the canvas? A task of this length would be quite tedious to program (100 lines of code!) Fortunately, Processing (like all programming languages) provides a variety of efficiency structures. One such structure used to create repetition is called a **for** loop. The **for** loop creates a variable, that contains a sequence of numbers which can be plugged into whatever command needs repeating. Up until now, the variables we declared were considered "global variables" since they were declared at the top and accessible throughout the entire program. In the case of a **for** loop, the variables are usually placed "locally," which means they are only accessible to the code within the **for** loop's brackets. Run the following program:

```
1   void setup() {
2   size(400, 150);
3   }
4
5   void draw() {
6   background(50,10,50);
7
8   //a for loop is defined by 3 parts
9   //variable; limit; assignment operator
10  for (int i = 0; i <= 400; i += 25){
11
12  //code to execute using the for loop variable "i"
13  fill (255,0,0);
14  ellipse (i,75,25,100);
15    }
16
17  }//close draw
18
```

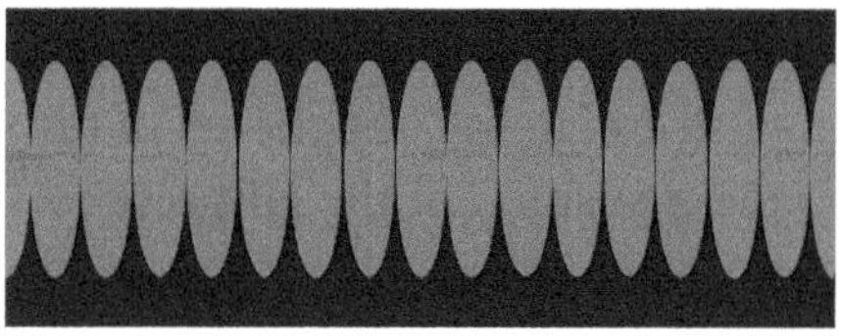

FIGURE 7.10

Previously, it would have required 17 lines of code to program 17 **ellipses**(). But, the **for** loop achieves the same results in about 3 lines of code. To strategically implement a **for** loop, it is critical to understand the 3 parts that define its parameters.

TABLE 7.2   Defining the 3 Parameters of a For Loop

Part Name	Variable	Limit	Assignment Operator
Explanation:	The variable holds the set of repetitions. It is declared and initialized at a starting value of your choice. (It is common to see these variables named "i" or "j".)	Here we specify the final possible value in the repetitive sequence.	This mathematical operation works on the variable to generate a series of new values until the limit is reached. (This part is often written in shorthand, see Figure 6.18).
Example: (from code line 10, Figure 7.10)	int i = 0; The first value in the repetition series is 0.	i <= 400; The last possible value in the repetition series is 400.	i += 25; Iterations of the variable "i" are produced incrementally by 25. So, her we have: 0, 25, 50, 75, 100...400.

The three parts that define a **for** loop are separated by semicolons and enclosed in parentheses. Once the **for** loop is defined, the variable generated by the **for** loop can be plugged into the code commands you want iterated (as long as the commands are contained within the **for** loop's curly brackets). In Figure 7.10, the set of numbers contained in "i" are plugged into the x position of the **ellipse()** command, thus drawing a horizontal series of 17 ellipses. Once completed, the **for** loop exits.

Like any other variable, we can plug a **for** loop variable into a variety of functions and arguments. Run the following program:

```
1   void setup() {
2   size(250, 250);
3   }
4
5   void draw() {
6   background(50,10,50);
7   rectMode (CENTER);
8
9   //1) start "i" at 255;
10  //2) limit "i" to stay above 0;
11  //3) iterate "i" by subtracting 25
12  for (int i = 255; i >= 0; i -= 25){
13
14  //use "i" for repetitive variations in color and size.
15  fill (i,i,0);
16  rect (125,125,i,i);
17  println (i); //verify "i" values in console
18    }
19
20  }//close draw
```

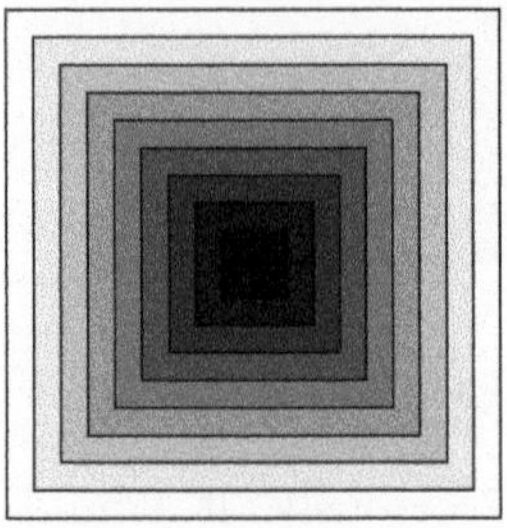

FIGURE 7.11

In Figure 7.11, we plug the **for** loop variable "i" into **fill()** and **rect()** to produce a sequence of rectangles in decreasing size and color. To verify the values a **for** loop produces, we use the **println()** function.

Another important note about **for** loops is that they must have an exit condition (a viable limit). Otherwise, the **for** loop will behave as an infinite loop and possibly crash your program. The following table contains some examples of infinite loops.

TABLE 7.3   Infinite Loop Examples

Expression	Problem
```for (int i = 25; i <= 0; i += 50){ //code to execute }```	The limit i<=0 is never possible because "i" starts at 25 and counts up by increments of 50. This loop has no exit condition and will loop infinitely.
```for (int i = 300; i >= 350; i -= 50){ //code to execute }```	The limit i >=350 is never possible because "i" starts at 300 and counts down by decrements of 50. This loop has no exit condition and will loop infinitely.

Another powerful use of a **for** loop is to nest one **for** loop inside of another. This creates a matrix of values, which can be used for gridded designs. Run the following program:

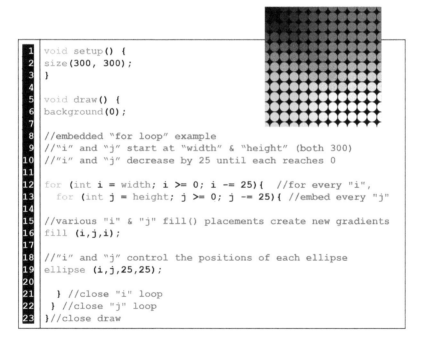

```
1   void setup() {
2   size(300, 300);
3   }
4
5   void draw() {
6   background(0);
7
8   //embedded "for loop" example
9   //"i" and "j" start at "width" & "height" (both 300)
10  //"i" and "j" decrease by 25 until each reaches 0
11
12  for (int i = width; i >= 0; i -= 25){  //for every "i",
13    for (int j = height; j >= 0; j -= 25){ //embed every "j"
14
15  //various "i" & "j" fill() placements create new gradients
16  fill (i,j,i);
17
18  //"i" and "j" control the positions of each ellipse
19  ellipse (i,j,25,25);
20
21    } //close "i" loop
22  } //close "j" loop
23  }//close draw
```

FIGURE 7.12

By inserting a second **for** loop inside of the first one, a matrix is created that generates every "j" to every "i". This strategy is fun for creating colorful gradients. As you advance in your programming studies, you will find that there are many more possibilities for using loops.

Exercise 7.3

Program a 250 × 250 pixel canvas with an embedded **for** loop of rectangles (50 × 50 pixels) that cover the canvas in the gradient colors of your choice. Multiple answers possible.

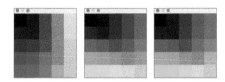

FIGURE 7.13

LESSON 7.4: COLOR DETECTION WITH FOR LOOPS

In Lesson 5.7, we explored color detection with the **get()** command. The following example is a review on how color detection works but this time implemented with a **for** loop. Run the following program:

```
float findcolor = 0;

void setup() {
size (300,300);
}

void draw() {
background (252,181,0);
noStroke();

//draw a grid of white ellipses with an embedded for loop
for (int i = 30 ; i <= width; i+=60){
   for (int j = 30 ; j <= height; j+=60){
   fill (255);
   ellipse (i,j,50,50);
   }
   }

//the variable "findcolor" is initialized with the get()
command, get() reports color values of the mouse position.
findcolor = get(mouseX, mouseY);


//println() reports the "findcolor" values in the console.
println ("color value=",findcolor);


//if the mouse is on white, show text on the canvas.
if (findcolor == -1.0 ) {
fill (0);
textSize (15);
textAlign (CENTER,CENTER);
text ("YOU ARE TOUCHING THE WHITE",width/2,height/2);
}
}//close draw
```

FIGURE 7.14

Color detection offers a variety of opportunities for game styled interactions and we will apply more complexity with this technique moving
forward.

Exercise 7.4

The following starter code uses the **random()** function inside of two *separate* **for** loops to create blue and green animated obstacles. There are also
two **text()** reports shown on the canvas of the variables: "detectblue" and
"detectgreen." First, run the starter code to see the line animations, then
program the following additions:

a. Write a conditional **if** statement that adds 1 to the "detectblue" variable whenever the mouse is over blue.

b. Create a similar detection/report for the green lines.

```
1   float findcolor = 0;
2   int detectblue = 0;
3   int detectgreen = 0;
4
5   void setup() {
6   size (400,400);
7   }
8
9   void draw() {
10  background(0);
11  strokeWeight (5);
12
13  for (int i=50; i < 350; i+=15){
14  stroke (0,0,255);
15  line (i,0, i, random(180,200));
16  }
17
18  for (int i=50; i < 350; i+=15){
19  stroke (0,255,0);
20  line (i,400, i ,random(200,220));
21  }
22
23
24  textSize (20);
25  fill (0,0,255);
26  text (detectblue, 350,100);
27  fill (0,255,0);
28  text (detectgreen, 350,300);
29
30  }//close draw
```

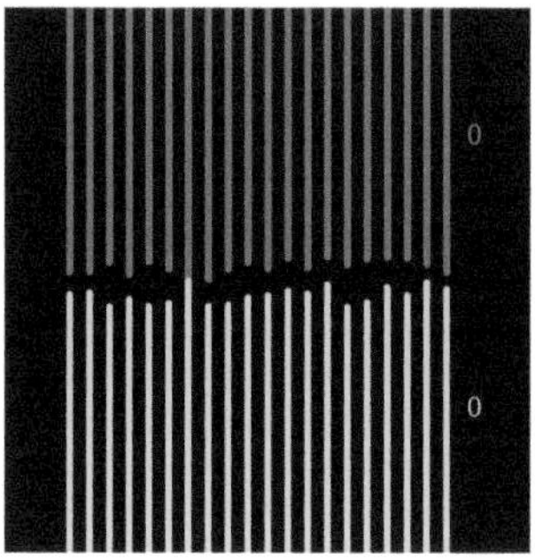

FIGURE 7.15

LESSON 7.5: GAME CREATION FROM KEYS, LOOPS, AND COLOR DETECTION

The following example implements a keyboard control system that moves a pink **rect()** as the player. An embedded **for** loop is used to generate a grid of looping, black ellipses that function as obstacles to the player. The rest of the program uses color detection to see collisions between the pink **rect()** and the black obstacles. A collisions report is displayed on the canvas by a "lives" variable. Run the following program:

```
//global variables
int x=100; //player position x
int y=100; //player position y
int directionX = 0; //horizontal directional control
int directionY = 0; //vertical directional control
int playerspeed= 3; //speed of player controlled by keys
int obstaclesMove = 0;
int lives = 0;

void setup(){
size(400, 400);
}

void draw(){
background(255,255,0);

//pink rectangular player
fill (255,0,255);
noStroke();
rectMode (CENTER);
rect (x, y, 20, 20);

//player movement (see lesson 7.2 for details)
x = x + (playerspeed * directionX);
y = y + (playerspeed * directionY);

//ellipse obstacles generated by an embedded for loop
//"i" values= -50,50,150,250,350: plugged into x position.
//"j" values=  50, 150, 250, 350: plugged into y position.
//"i" + "obstaclesMove" creates looping animation
for (int i = -50; i < width+50; i += 100){
  for (int j = 50; j < height; j += 100){
    fill (0);
    ellipse (i+obstaclesMove,j,50,50);
  }
}

//code continued in next figure
```

FIGURE 7.16   Code example continued in Figures 7.17–7.18.

```
39   // "obstaclesMove" assignment operator & reset
40   // (both located outside of the for loop so that
41   // they act on the entire variable set "i" simultaneously)
42      obstaclesMove = obstaclesMove + 1;
43      if (obstaclesMove > 50) {
44        obstaclesMove= -50;
45      }
46
47   //collisions report
48      fill (0);
49      textAlign (CENTER,CENTER);
50      textSize (14);
51      text ("lives="+lives, 40, 15); //"label"+variable, x, y
52
53   //detect color on all 4 sides of the player
54   //"x" and "y" are in the center of the 20x20 rect()
55   //so, an 11 pixel offset activates the 4 edges
56      int side1 = get(x-11, y-11);
57      int side2 = get(x+11, y-11);
58      int side3 = get(x-11, y+11);
59      int side4 = get(x+11, y+11);
60
61   //color detection reports black value as -1.6777216E7
62      float findcolor = get (mouseX,mouseY);
63      println (findcolor);
64
65   //collision: if any side of the player detects black...
66      if((side1 == -1.6777216E7)||
67        (side2 == -1.6777216E7)||
68        (side3 == -1.6777216E7)||
69        (side4 == -1.6777216E7)){ //then
70        x = 100; //reset x position
71        y = 100; //reset y position
72        directionX= 0; //x stop moving
73        directionY= 0; //y stop moving
74        lives = lives - 1; //subtract one from "lives"
75      }
76   } //close draw
77
78
79   //code continued in next figure
```

FIGURE 7.17   Code example continued in Figure 7.18.

```
80  // keyboard controls (see lesson 7.2 for details)
81  void keyPressed() {
82
83      if (keyCode == LEFT){
84        directionX= -1; //x go left
85        directionY= 0; //y stop
86      }
87      else if (keyCode == RIGHT){
88        directionX= 1; //x go right
89        directionY= 0; //y stop
90      }
91      else if (keyCode == UP){
92        directionX= 0; //x stop
93        directionY= -1; //y go up
94      }
95      else if (keyCode == DOWN){
96        directionX= 0; //x stop
97        directionY= 1; //y go down
98      }
99      else if (keyCode == SHIFT){
100       directionX= 0; //x stop
101       directionY= 0; //y stop
102     }
103 }//close keyPressed
```

FIGURE 7.18

As you can see, intricate procedures produce longer programs. Annotations and organization is key to navigating these more lengthy projects. Below are a few follow-up notes to further unpack this example.

TABLE 7.4   Key Notes for Program Example (Figures 7.16–7.18).

Code Lines	Subject	Notes
1–8	global variables	These variables are placed globally so they can be accessed by multiple parts of the program.
27–45	**for** loops vs the looping in **void draw()**	The variable named "obstaclesMove" is added to "i" inside of the embedded **for** loop. But, further down, we see the "obstaclesMove" assignment operator and reset *outside* of the embedded **for** loop. This placement is due to the behavior of a **for** loop. A **for** loop does its entire repetition sequence within *one cycle* of **void draw()**. If the assignment operator and reset were placed inside of the embedded **for** loop, then they would execute 20 times faster to account for every value in the **for** loop variable cycle. "i" values = −50, 50, 150, 250, 350 "j" values = 50, 150, 250, 350 "i" * "j"= 20 repetitions

By placing the assignment operator and reset for "obstaclesMove" outside of the **for** loop, the program executes these commands once per each cycle of **void draw()** and the animation runs at a more desirable pace.

(Continued)

TABLE 7.4 (Continued)   Key Notes for Program Example (Figures 7.16–7.18).

Code Lines	Subject	Notes
51	**text()** command variations	To display custom labels next to the value of a variable shown on the canvas, use the following syntax for the **text()** command: text ("text you want to display" + variable name, x, y);
53–59	4 sided color detection	In this color detection example, our 20 × 20 pink **rect()** covers a much larger region than the mouse cursor we used in prior examples. We also now have *moving* obstacles, which could touch any side of the pink **rect()**. For accurate collision detection, we need to program a color detection that covers all four sides of the **rect()**. So, color detection is set at 11 pixels from the center of every side of the **rect()**.

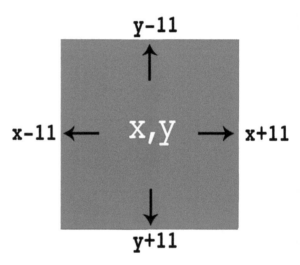

56–59, 62	local variables	Each one of these variables are initialized inside of **void draw()** with fluctuating values pulled from the **get()** command. These variables are not needed outside of **void draw()**, so it is most efficient to declare and initialize them locally.
66–69	syntax legibility	Here we see a lengthy, conjoined conditional statement spread over 4 lines to create better legibility. As long as your syntax is correct, spreading longer statements over several lines of code should work fine.

Exercise 7.5

FIGURE 7.19

a. Add a conditional **if** statement inside of **void draw()**, that displays "YOU WIN" on the canvas whenever the pink rectangle crosses the bottom boundary of the canvas.

b. Add a second conditional **if** statement inside of **void draw()**, that displays "GAME OVER" on the canvas whenever the "lives" variable is equivalent to 0.

LESSON 7.6: IMAGE COLLISIONS WITH THE DISTANCE() FUNCTION

FIGURE 7.20

When an image contains several colors, color detection may prove unreliable for collisions. The **dist()** function detects the amount of space between two points – so, color doesn't matter. In the following example, the arrow keys are used to control a player dodging two falling enemies. A yellow health bar shrinks each time the **dist()** function detects an intersection between the player and an enemy. To get started on this example, download the folder: "Chapter 7 Lesson Imagery" and import the images "player.png", "enemy.png", and "place.png". Place the images inside of a data folder (see Lesson 4.1 for more info on loading images) and run the following program.

```
1  //image variables
2  PImage enemy;
3  PImage place;
4  PImage player;
5
6  //player movement variables
7  float playerX = 50; //player position x
8  float playerY = 475; //player position y
9  int directionX = 0; //horizontal direction
10 float playerSpeed = 5;
11
12 //enemy movement variables
13 float enemyLX = 150; //leftside enemy
14 float enemyLY = 200; //"
15 float enemyRX = 450; //rightside enemy
16 float enemyRY = 200; //"
17 float enemySpeed = 5;
18 int health = 150;
19
20 void setup(){
21 size(600,600);
22 player = loadImage("player.png");
23 enemy = loadImage("enemy.png");
24 place = loadImage("place.png");
25 }
26
27 void draw(){
28 background (0);
29 imageMode(CENTER);
30 image (place, width/2,height/2,600,600);//background image
31
32 //health bar
33 fill (230,218,29);
34 noStroke();
35 rect (0,0,25,health);//health bar height starts at 150
36
37 //player
38 image(player,playerX, playerY);
39
40 //player keyboard movement (see lesson 7.2)
41 playerX = playerX + (playerSpeed * directionX);
42
43 //code continued in next figure
```

FIGURE 7.21 Code example continued in Figure 7.22).

```
44  //player reset
45  if (playerX > 650){ //if the player passes the right side
46  playerX = 50;          //then reset the player's x position
47  directionX= 0;         //and stop the player's movement
48  }
49
50  //left side enemy
51  image(enemy, enemyLX, enemyLY);
52  enemyLY = enemyLY + enemySpeed; //move down
53  if(enemyLY > 700){//if left enemy is off-screen (bottom)
54  enemyLY = -150;       //then reset it back to the top
55  enemyLX = random(150,300);//and randomize the x position
56  }
57
58  //right side enemy
59  image(enemy, enemyRX, enemyRY);
60  enemyRY = enemyRY - enemySpeed; //move up
61  if(enemyRY < -100){//if right enemy is off-screen (top)
62  enemyRY = 750;         //then reset it back to the bottom
63  enemyRX = random(300,600);//and randomize the x position
64  }
65
66  //collision
67  //if the distance between the player and the left side
68  //enemy is less than 100
69  //or, " for the right side enemy
70  if ((dist(playerX,playerY,enemyLX,enemyLY) < 100) ||
71      (dist(playerX,playerY,enemyRX,enemyRY) < 100)) {
72  playerX = 50;          //then reset player's x position
73  directionX = 0;        //stop player's motion
74  health = health - 50; //reduce the size of the health bar
75  }
76
77  } //close draw
78
79  //horizontal keyboard controls (see lesson 7.2)
80  void keyPressed() {
81      if (keyCode == LEFT){
82      directionX= -1; //go left
83      }
84      else if (keyCode == RIGHT){
85      directionX= 1; //go right
86      }
87  }//close keyPressed
```

FIGURE 7.22

The following table unpacks this example in depth.

TABLE 7.5   Notes on Program Example (Figures 7.21–7.22).

Code Lines	Subject	Notes
2, 4, 66–71	**dist()** function collisions	The **dist()** function measures the distance between 2 points.

		Although a design may have an odd shape, if it is a .png with a transparent background, it still reads as a rectangular shape. When using the **dist()** function for collision detection on all 4 sides, consider using images that fit well in an evenly sized box. These images will produce the most visibly accurate collisions. In this example, both the player and enemy are 100 × 100 pixels in size, so the distance from their center anchor points to each side is 50. When the player and enemy intersect, their **dist()** is roughly 100 (50 + 50). These collisions are not perfect but pretty close! Finesse your values as you see fit.
32–35, 74	health bar	The health bar is a simple yellow **rect()** with an integer variable controlling the height of the **rect()**. In this case, **rectMode (CENTER)** is *not* used because we want the health bar to shrink in one direction rather than equally from the center. Every time the player collides with an enemy, 50 pixels are subtracted from the height of the **rect()**.
55, 63	randomized enemy positions	To spice the game up, a **random()** number is plugged into the horizontal positions of each enemy. These positions change every time the enemies are reset to the top of the screen.

Exercise 7.6

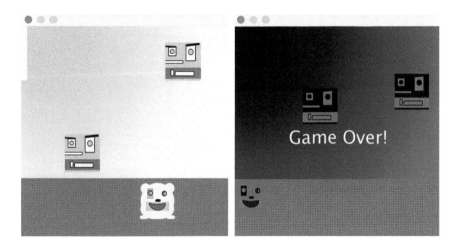

FIGURE 7.23

Building on the example from Figure 7.23,

a. Add an assignment operator that acts on the "enemySpeed" variable so that it increases by 5 every time the player passes the right side.

b. Write a conditional **if** statement that implements the **tint()** function in red and prints the text, "game over" whenever the "health" variable becomes 0 or less. (See Lesson 4.3 for a review on the **tint()** function.)

LESSON 7.7: TWO PLAYERS, DIRECTIONAL MOVEMENT, AND JUMPING!

FIGURE 7.24

Now, we will program a two-player skateboarding game which keeps the orientation of an image consistent with the characters' movements and gives users the ability to make the skaters jump. From the download folder: "Chapter 7 Lesson Imagery", import the following images inside of a data folder:

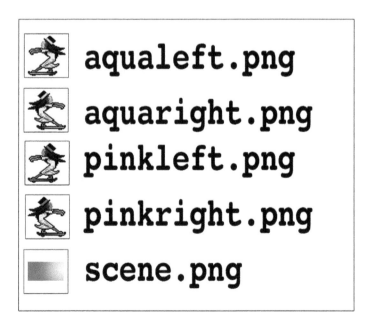

FIGURE 7.25

Now, run the following program:

```
1   //movement variables
2   int aquaX = 200;
3   int aquaY = 425;
4
5   int pinkX = 800;
6   int pinkY = 425;
7
8   //boolean switches controlled by keyPressed()
9   boolean leftaqua = false;  //key a = left
10  boolean rightaqua = false; //key d = right
11  boolean jumpaqua = false;  //key w = jump
12
13  boolean leftpink = false;  //key j = left
14  boolean rightpink = false; //key l = right
15  boolean jumppink =false;   //key i = jump
16
17  //image variables
18  PImage aquaR; //facing right
19  PImage aquaL; //facing left
20  int aquaOri = 1; //image orientation
21
22  PImage pinkR; //facing right
23  PImage pinkL; //facing left
24  int pinkOri = 2; //image orientation
25
26  PImage gradient; //background
27
28  void setup(){
29  size (1000,500);
30  gradient = loadImage("scene.png");
31  aquaR = loadImage("aquaright.png");
32  aquaL = loadImage("aqualeft.png");
33  pinkR = loadImage("pinkright.png");
34  pinkL = loadImage("pinkleft.png");
35  }
36
37  void draw(){
38  background(255);
39  imageMode(CENTER);
40  image (gradient, width/2, height/2);
41
42
43  //code continued in next figure
```

FIGURE 7.26   Code example continued in Figures 7.27–7.29.

```
44  //image display & orientation
45  if (aquaOri == 1){
46  image(aquaR,aquaX,aquaY); //right facing
47  }
48  else if (aquaOri == 2){
49  image(aquaL,aquaX,aquaY); //left facing
50  }
51  if (pinkOri == 1){
52  image(pinkR,pinkX,pinkY); //right facing
53  }
54  else if (pinkOri == 2){
55  image(pinkL,pinkX,pinkY); //left facing
56  }
57
58  ////aqua skater movement control////
59
60  //"d" key controls right
61  if (rightaqua){ //if true
62  aquaX = aquaX + 5; //move right
63  aquaOri = 1;//orientation state = 1(right)
64  }
65
66  //"a" key controls left
67  if (leftaqua){ //if true
68  aquaX = aquaX - 5; //move left
69  aquaOri = 2;//orientation state = 2(left)
70  }
71
72  //"w" key controls jumping
73  if (jumpaqua==true && aquaOri==1){//if true & right
74  aquaY = aquaY - 10; //jump
75  aquaX = aquaX + 4; //to the right
76  }
77  else if (jumpaqua==true && aquaOri==2){//if true & left
78  aquaY = aquaY - 10; //jump
79  aquaX = aquaX - 4; //to the left
80  }
81
82  //reset jumps
83  if (aquaY < 50){
84  aquaY = 425;
85  jumpaqua = false;
86  }
87  //code continued in next figure
```

FIGURE 7.27   Code example continued in Figures 7.28–7.29.

```
88  ////pink skater movement control////
89
90  //"l" key controls right
91  if (rightpink){ //if true
92  pinkX = pinkX + 5; //move right
93  pinkOri = 1; //image orientation = 1 (right)
94  }
95
96  // "j" key controls left
97  if (leftpink){ //if true
98  pinkX = pinkX - 5; //move left
99  pinkOri = 2; //image orientation = 2 (left)
100 }
101
102 //"i" key controls jump
103 if (jumppink==true && pinkOri==1){ //if true & right
104 pinkY = pinkY - 10; //jump
105 pinkX = pinkX + 4; //to the right
106 }
107 else if (jumppink==true && pinkOri==2){//if true & left
108 pinkY = pinkY - 10; //jump
109 pinkX = pinkX - 4; //to the left
110 }
111
112 //reset jumps
113 if (pinkY < 50){
114 pinkY = 425;
115 jumppink = false;
116 }
117 } //close draw
118
119 void keyPressed(){ ////turns booleans on////
120
121 //aqua skater
122 if (key == 'a' || key == 'A'){       //left
123 leftaqua=true;
124 }
125 else if(key == 'd' || key == 'D'){ //right
126 rightaqua=true;
127 }
128 else if(key == 'w'|| key == 'W'){   //jump
129 jumpaqua=true;
130 }
131 //code continued in next figure
```

FIGURE 7.28 Code example continued in Figure 7.29.

```
132  //pink skater
133  if (key == 'j'|| key == 'J'){ //left
134  leftpink=true;
135  }
136  else if(key == 'l' || key == 'L'){  //right
137  rightpink=true;
138  }
139  else if(key == 'i' || key == 'I'){ //jump
140  jumppink=true;
141  }
142  } //close keyPressed()
143
144
145  void keyReleased(){ ////turns booleans off////
146
147  //aqua skater
148  if(key == 'a' || key == 'A'){
149  leftaqua=false;
150  }
151  else if(key == 'd'|| key == 'D'){
152  rightaqua=false;
153  }
154
155  //pink skater
156  if(key == 'j' || key == 'J'){
157  leftpink=false;
158  }
159  else if(key == 'l' || key == 'L'){
160  rightpink=false;
161  }
162  } //close keyReleased()
```

FIGURE 7.29

TABLE 7.6   Notes on Program Example (Figures 7.26–7.29)

Code Line	Subject	Notes
20, 24, 44–56	state variables	Up until now, we have used integers to count up or count down for animations, but here we use the integer variables, "aquaOri" and "pinkOri" as *state* variables. Depending on what number these variables become – a different state will be executed. In this particular example, both of these variables determine which orientation the photo should be facing (one for the aqua skater image and the other for the pink skater). If either of their values becomes 1, then the state is right facing. If their values are 2, then the state is left facing.
58–70, 88–100, 119–127, 132–142, 145–162	horizontal keyboard movements	The keys "a" and "d'" control the directional travel of the aqua skater and the keys "j" and "l" control the same for the pink skater. This time we use booleans to control motion in increments of 5 (rather than the continuous motion shown in an earlier example.) These movements are initiated with **keyPressed**() and stopped with **keyReleased**(). Depending on your machine, the key buttons may behave differently.
72–86, 102–116, 128–130, 139–141	jumping keyboard movements	The keys "w" and "i" control when the skaters jump. If the booleans "jumpaqua" and "jumppink" become **true**, the skaters are propelled up and over in their respective directions. Traveling upwards means that y values are getting smaller. When the skaters' y-axis variables become less than 50 (almost to the top of the screen), they are then reset back to their ground position of 425 and turned **false**.

Exercise 7.7

FIGURE 7.30

a. Each skater image is 150 × 150 pixels in size. Program a collision using the **dist()** function that resets each skater back to their starting position whenever they intersect.

b. Create a scoreboard for each skater on the canvas that tracks and adds a point whenever one passes the other and makes it to the other side.

We have now concluded this chapter on simple techniques for video game design. The next and final chapter of this book provides a variety of multilevel architectures for creating more complex projects. The templates within Chapter 8 combined with the lessons from Chapters 1 to 7 should provide you with enough ideas and strategies to create an original and interactively fun, master project.

As previously mentioned, several unique and innovative student projects based on the lessons from this book are available for download at the end of Chapter 8.

FIGURE 7.31   Student project example: interactive makeover simulation. (Printed with permission from Kathryn Wylie.)

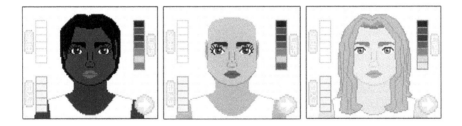

FIGURE 7.32   Student project example: variations of interactive makeover simulation. (Printed with permission from Kathryn Wylie.)

CHAPTER 8

Multilevel Architectures and Arrays

FIGURE 8.1   Student project example: multilevel, escape room game. (Printed with permission from Sierra Gillingham.)

In this last chapter, we will use variable collections and level structures to create multilayered, interactive experiences. The lessons presented in this chapter are meant to provide organizational structures that can be

FIGURE 8.2   Student project example: multilevel, escape room game. (Printed with permission from Sierra Gillingham.)

interwoven with any of the examples presented in this book. Your last assignment will be to make a master project of your choice. Depending on your interests, this could manifest as a combat game, an interactive mystery, a visual design program, a choice-based quiz, or? Examples of these types of projects and many more creative expressions are provided in the downloads folder for this chapter (available on the publisher's website). Let's get started!

LESSON 8.1: BASIC LEVELS ARCHITECTURE

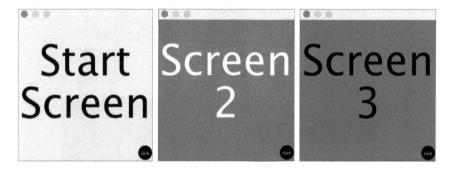

FIGURE 8.3

In this example, we will create a series of screens that change every time a button is clicked. The code here should feel familiar. What's different is how the elements are combined. Run the following program:

```
1   int screen=1;      //used for changing screens
2   int c = 0;         //used in text animation for level 2
3   int move = 250;    //used in text animation for level 3
4
5   void setup () {
6   size (500,500);
7   }
8
9   void draw () {
10  textAlign (CENTER,CENTER);
11  println ("screen=",screen); //variable report
12
13
14  //screen 1
15  if (screen == 1) {
16  background (0,255,255);
17
18  //text design
19  fill (0);
20  textSize(150);
21  text("Start", 250, 125);
22  text("Screen", 250, 275);
23  } //close screen 1
24
25
26  //screen 2
27  if (screen == 2){
28  background(255,0,0);
29
30  //text design with color change from black to white
31  fill (c);
32  c = c + 3;
33  if (c>255){
34  c=255;
35  }
36  textSize(150);
37  text("Screen", 250, 125);
38  text("2", 250, 275);
39  } //close screen 2
40
41
42  //code continued in next figure
43
```

FIGURE 8.4   Code continued in Figure 8.5.

```
44  //screen 3
45  if (screen == 3){
46  background (0,0,255);
47
48  //text design moves right
49  fill (0);
50  textSize(150);
51  fill (0);
52  textSize(150);
53  text("Screen", move, 125);
54  text("3", move, 275);
55  move = move + 3;
56  } //close screen 3
57
58
59  //reset all variables to start over
60  if (screen == 4){
61  c = 0;
62  move = 250;
63  screen = 1;
64  } //close screen 4
65
66
67  //button design displays on top of all screens
68  fill (0);
69  ellipse (470,470,50,50);
70  fill (255);
71  textSize(14);
72  text("click", 470, 470);
73  } //close draw
74
75
76  //screens change when the mouse is pressed on button region
77  void mousePressed() {
78  if((mouseX>400) &&
79  (mouseX<500) &&
80  (mouseY>400) &&
81  (mouseY<500)){
82  screen = screen + 1;
83  }
84  }//close mousePressed
```

FIGURE 8.5

TABLE 8.1 Notes on Program Example (Figures 8.4–8.5).

Code Lines:	Subject:	Notes:
1, 15, 45, 60, 63, 82	screen changing variable	We use an **int** named "screen" to function as a state variable. Previously, we used integer variables for animations and counting sequences. Here, we use an integer variable for specifying states of activity such as screen levels. The "screen" variable changes when the **mousePressed()** function adds 1 to it.
67–72	button activated	Displayed at the end of **void draw()** is the button design. But, the button display is only a visual cue to tell the user where to click. It is the conditional within **mousePressed()** that actually checks to see if the button region was pressed. Also, note that since the button is displayed on every screen, it only needs to be drawn once after all of the screens inside of **void draw()**.
59–64	reset and restart	All of the variable values are changed by the time the third "screen" loads. In order to make the whole system repeatable when it is restarted, we reset these variables back to their original values inside of "screen" 4.

Exercise 8.1

FIGURE 8.6

In the previous example, the reset "screen" is 4. Change it to 5 and make a new "screen" 4 with the following details:

  a. Program the new "screen" 4 with a green background and white letters that read: "Screen 4".

  b. Animate the text line "Screen" to move up and the number "4" to move down.

  c. Update the variables inside the reset "screen" 5, so that all the whole system is repeatable with all animations intact.

LESSON 8.2: STATES WITHIN LEVELS

FIGURE 8.7

In this example, we will move a sea turtle through various ocean backgrounds. From the download folder: "Chapter 8 Lesson Imagery", import the following images inside of a data folder.

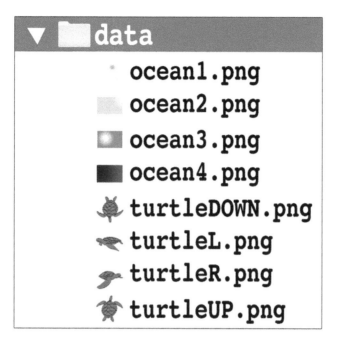

FIGURE 8.8

Now, run the following program.

```
1   //state variables
2   int level = 1;
3   int state = 0;
4
5   //movement variables
6   int x1 = 300;
7   int y1 = 250;
8   int speed = 0;
9
10  //image variables
11  PImage turtleL;
12  PImage turtleR;
13  PImage turtleUP;
14  PImage turtleDOWN;
15  PImage ocean1;
16  PImage ocean2;
17  PImage ocean3;
18  PImage ocean4;
19
20  void setup(){
21  size(600,400);
22  turtleL = loadImage ("turtleL.png");
23  turtleR = loadImage ("turtleR.png");
24  turtleUP = loadImage ("turtleUP.png");
25  turtleDOWN = loadImage ("turtleDOWN.png");
26  ocean1 = loadImage ("ocean1.png");
27  ocean2 = loadImage ("ocean2.png");
28  ocean3 = loadImage ("ocean3.png");
29  ocean4 = loadImage ("ocean4.png");
30  }
31
32  void draw(){
33  imageMode (CENTER);
34
35  //variable reports
36  println("x1=", x1);
37  println("y1=", y1);
38  println ("level=", level);
39  println ("state=", state);
40
41
42
43  //code continued in next figure
```

FIGURE 8.9 Code continued in Figures 8.10–8.11.

```
44  //level 1
45  if (level == 1) {
46  image(ocean1, width/2, height/2);
47  fill (0,100);
48  textSize (20);
49  text ("Level 1", 10, 380);
50  textSize (12);
51  text ("Use Arrow Keys and Shift", 10, 395);
52  } //close level 1
53
54
55  //level 2
56  if (level == 2) {
57  image(ocean2, width/2, height/2);
58  fill(0,100);
59  textSize (20);
60  text ("Level 2", 10,380);
61  } //close level 2
62
63
64  //level 3
65  if (level == 3) {
66  image(ocean3, width/2, height/2);
67  fill(0,100);
68  text ("Level 3", 10,380);
69  } //close level 3
70
71
72  //level 4
73  if (level == 4) {
74  image(ocean4, width/2, height/2);
75  fill(255,100);
76  text ("Level 4", 10,380);
77  } //close level 4
78
79
80  //reset
81  if (level == 5){
82  level = 1;
83  state = 0;
84  x1 = 300;
85  } //close reset
86
87  //code continued in next figure
```

FIGURE 8.10   Code continued in Figure 8.11.

```
88  //differents states of movement
89     if (state == 0) { //up orientation & no movement
90     image(turtleUP, x1, y1);
91     speed = 0;
92     }
93     else if (state == 1) { //left orientation & movement
94     image(turtleL, x1, y1);
95     speed = 2;
96     x1 = x1 - speed;
97     }
98     else if (state == -1) {//right orientation & movement
99     image(turtleR, x1, y1);
100    speed = 2;
101    x1 = x1 + speed;
102    }
103
104
105 //moving off screen changes levels & reverses direction
106    if ((x1 < -50) || (x1 > 650)){
107    level = level + 1;
108    state = state * -1;
109    }
110 }   //close draw
111
112
113 //keyboard assignments for each state
114    void keyPressed(){
115    if ( keyCode == SHIFT ) {
116    state = 0;
117    }
118    else if ( keyCode == LEFT ) {
119    state = 1;
120    }
121    else if ( keyCode == RIGHT ) {
122    state = -1;
123    }
124 } //close keyPressed
```

FIGURE 8.11

TABLE 8.2   Notes on Program Example (Figures 8.9–8.11).

Code Lines:	Subject:	Notes:
7, 14, 25	inactive variable/ image	These code lines are set up in preparation for Exercise 8.2.
1–3	state variables	Throughout the program we use these two different integer variables. The variable "level" triggers changes to the ocean backgrounds whenever the turtle crosses a side. The variable "state" determines the turtle's orientation and directional movement.
88–102, 113–124	keyboard controls over turtle	In **mousePressed**(), we assign each "state" of turtle's movements to a specific key. In lines 88–102, we initialize each state with a direction and image orientation for the turtle.
105–109	levels change turtle direction	Here, we have set up a conditional that checks to see if the turtle's x-axis variable has crossed either side of the screen. When it does, the "level" variable changes and the turtle's direction is reversed. This is because the "state" variable is multiplied by −1 whenever it reaches a boundary. (See Lesson 5.6 for a review of alternating directional movement.)
80–85	reset and restart	Here, we reset all variables back to their initial values for a perfect restart whenever "level" becomes 5.

Exercise 8.2

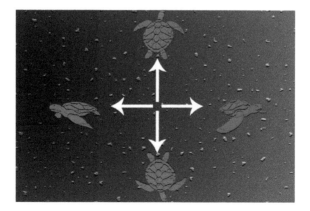

FIGURE 8.12

Add onto the previous example so that the turtle now moves with all *four* arrow keys to all *four* sides of the canvas causing a level change whenever *any* side is crossed. Make sure the correct image orientation is loaded for each "state" and that when a "level" is changed, the turtle reverses its direction. Don't forget to reset the turtle's y-axis position whenever the "level" goes back to 1.

LESSON 8.3: ARRAYS

Another efficiency structure commonly used in programming is the **array[]**. Identified by square brackets, an **array[]** is a *set* of same-type variables (integers, floats, booleans, images, etc.). Until now, we programmed single variables stacked up, one at a time in our projects. But, the **array[]** structure can hold large collections of variables in one container. For example, instead of declaring and initializing 15 **float** variables separately, we could declare one **array[]** to hold all 15 **float** variables at once. The **array[]** structure is not only useful for writing programs more economically but it also provides new design and functionality opportunities. As with variables, an **array[]** can be declared, initialized, and implemented in a variety of ways. To start our investigation, run the following program:

```
1    //int array[] named "Myset" initialized with 6 values
2    int[] Myset = new int[] {15,75,123,105,165,290};
3
4    void setup (){
5    size (100,100);
6    }
7
8    void draw () {
9
10   //each value in an array[] is assigned an index number
11   //indexes always start at 0
12   //indices for the 6 values in mySet[] are: 0,1,2,3,4,5
13
14
15   //println()confirms the values assigned to each indices
16   println ("index position 0=",Myset[0]); //refers to 15
17   println ("index position 1=",Myset[1]); //refers to 75
18   println ("index position 2=",Myset[2]); //refers to 123
19   println ("index position 3=",Myset[3]); //refers to 105
20   println ("index position 4=",Myset[4]); //refers to 165
21   println ("index position 5=",Myset[5]); //refers to 290
22   }
```

FIGURE 8.13

In Figure 8.13, we see an **array[]** declared and initialized in one line of code. The syntax of an **array[]** is structured a bit differently when compared to single variables.

TABLE 8.3   Declaring and Initializing an Array in the Same Line of Code

Example:	int[]	Myset	=	new	int[]	{15,75,123,105,165,290};
Explanation:	Declare the array[] data type	Name the array[]	Assign the array[]	Write the keyword new	Repeat the array[] data type	Assign values to the array[] inside of curly brackets {}

Not every program requires an **array[]** to be declared and initialized in the same line of code. More on that later.

Another important aspect of understanding how an **array[]** works is, knowing the difference between the values held in an **array[]** and the index numbers that refer to these values. As shown in Figure 8.13, there is an index position assigned to every value in an **array[]**. Index values always start at 0. For example, an array containing 6 values has 6 index positions: 0,1,2,3,4,5. We use these index numbers to call certain values from an **array[]** for use in our programs. It is also important to note that if you try to call an index number that doesn't exist in the specified **array[]**, your program will come up with errors.

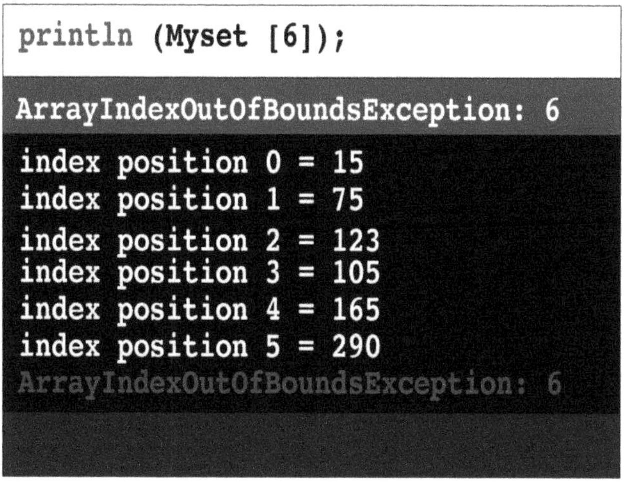

```
println (Myset [6]);

ArrayIndexOutOfBoundsException: 6

index position 0 = 15
index position 1 = 75
index position 2 = 123
index position 3 = 105
index position 4 = 165
index position 5 = 290
ArrayIndexOutOfBoundsException: 6
```

FIGURE 8.14   (The **array[]** called "MySet" contains 6 indices (0,1,2,3,4,5). Index number 6 called by **println()** is out of bounds.)

In this next example, we will use the same **array[]** from Figure 8.13 to vary the positions of 6 different ellipses. Run the following program:

```
1   int[] Myset = new int[] {15,75,123,105,165,290};
2
3   void setup (){
4   size (300,300);
5   }
6
7   void draw () {
8   background (208,236,237);
9   noStroke();
10  fill (100,0,100,100);
11
12  ellipse (Myset[0],150, 50, 200); //x position =  15
13  ellipse (Myset[1],150, 50, 200); //x position =  75
14  ellipse (Myset[2],150, 50, 200); //x position = 123
15  ellipse (Myset[3],150, 50, 200); //x position = 105
16  ellipse (Myset[4],150, 50, 200); //x position = 165
17  ellipse (Myset[5],150, 50, 200); //x position = 290
18  }
```

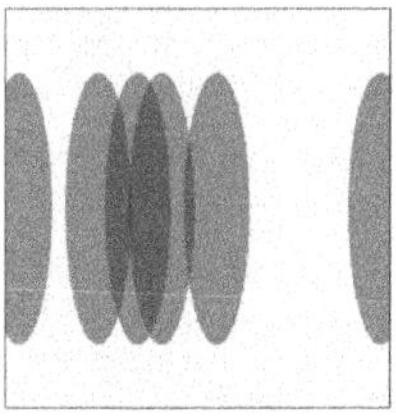

FIGURE 8.15

In Figure 8.15, each value of the **array[]** is plugged into an individual **ellipse()**. Depending on your project needs, this strategy may be necessary. However, this repetition of **ellipse()** commands can be streamlined. To reduce code redundancy, we can use the iterative power of a **for** loop to consolidate the program's access to all of the **array[]** values. The following example uses just one **ellipse()** command and a **for** loop to create a variable index. Run the program:

```
1   int[] Myset = new int[] {15,75,123,105,165,290};
2
3   void setup (){
4   size (300,300);
5   }
6
7   void draw () {
8   background (208,236,237);
9   noStroke();
10  fill (100,0,100,100);
11
12  for (int i = 0; i < 6; i++){   //"i" = 0,1,2,3,4,5
13  ellipse(Myset[i],150,50,200); //all "i" indices are applied
14  }
15  }
```

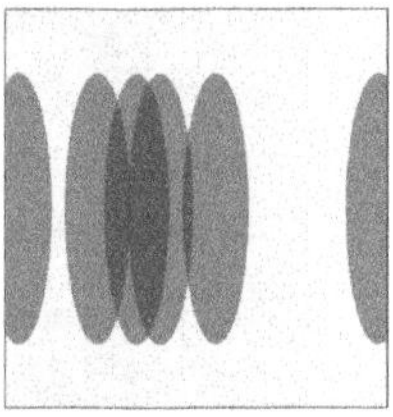

FIGURE 8.16

In Figure 8.16, the **for** loop is used to access each value in the **array** []
at once by creating a variable set called "i," that is identical to the array's
index. It is important to note that these two must be *identical*. If you generate a variable index for an **array**[] that is too large or contains numbers not
included in the original index, then your program will have errors. Once
you have a variable index generated by the **for** loop, you can plug it into
your **array**[] and apply the **array**[] where you need it. Therefore, in Figure
8.16, we applied the **array**[] of integers to the x position of the **ellipse**(). In
the next **array**[] example, we will expand on this strategy by initializing
an **array**[] with **random**() values every time the mouse is pressed. Run the
following example:

```
1   //array[] "x" is declared with 6 float values in its set
2   float[] x = new float [6];
3
4   void setup (){
5   size (250,250);
6   }
7
8   void draw () {
9   background (255);
10
11  //x[] values report
12  println("x[]="); //label
13  println(x); //report
14
15
16  //6 indices from x[] are assigned to "i"
17  for (int i = 0; i < 6; i = i + 1){
18  fill (x[i],0,0); //x[i] is applied to the red fill
19  ellipse ((x[i]),125, 100, 100); //" x position
20  }
21  }
22
23  //everytime the mouse is pressed
24  //initialize each indice with a random() value
25  void mousePressed(){
26  x[0] = random(255);
27  x[1] = random(255);
28  x[2] = random(255);
29  x[3] = random(255);
30  x[4] = random(255);
31  x[5] = random(255);
32  }
```

FIGURE 8.17

TABLE 8.4   Notes on Program Example (Figure 8.17).

Code Lines	Subject	Notes
1–2	**array**[] declared but not initialized in the same line of code	In this example, we declare a **new float array**[] with 6 values. But, we do not initialize these values until later in the program with **mousePressed**(). However, that does not mean the **array**[] starts off empty. By default, an **int** or **float array**[] will contain a set of zeros until initialized. That is why, when you first run this example, there are 6 black ellipses stacked on top of each other prior to the mouse being pressed. (Also, note that the default value of an **int** or **float** *variable* is 0, while booleans are false.)
11–13	**println**() with **arrays**[]	It is always beneficial to use **println**() to verify variables and this is no different for an **array**[]. If you only need information on one member of the array, then you can implement **println**() as demonstrated in Figure 8.13. However, if you want to access the whole **array**[] set more efficiently, it turns out that the **println**() command will organize an **array**[] report very nicely if you *only* put the **array**[] name in **println**(). If you need to label the **array**[] report, add a 2nd **println**() with the name of the **array**[] in quotes.
16–20	**for** loop array[] index	We use a **for** loop to create the index "i" for the "x" **array**[]. By plugging "i" into **x**[], all values of the **array**[] are called simultaneously. In this example, **x[i]** is applied to the red **fill**() and the x-axis position of the **ellipse**(). Thus generating 6 variations of color and placement.
23–32	**mousePresssed**() initializes the **array**[]	Every time the mouse is pressed, each indice for **x**[] is assigned a new **random**() **float** value.

Exercise 8.3

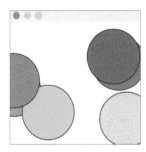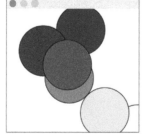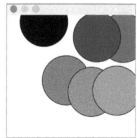

FIGURE 8.18

a. Building onto the previous example (Figure 8.18), by adding a second **array**[] called "y" that holds 6 **float** values and uses the same "i" index that the "x" **array**[] uses.

b. Next, plug **y[i]** into the green argument of **fill()** and the y-axis position of the **ellipse()**.

c. In **mousePressed()**, initialize each value in **y[]** to load a **random()** number.

LESSON 8.4: IMAGE ARRAYS

FIGURE 8.19

In this example, we will load an **array**[] with a sequence of images and use **mousePressed()** to trigger them to appear as stacking boxes. From the download folder: "Chapter 8 Lesson Imagery", import the following images inside of a data folder:

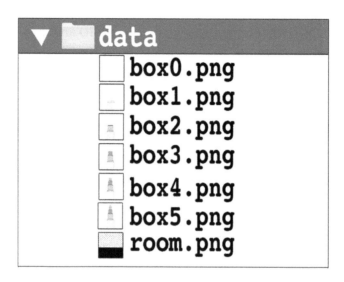

FIGURE 8.20

Please note that *all* of the .png images used in this example are 500 × 500 pixels with transparency. For this particular example, the images were all exported the exact same size as the canvas to create a perfect, symmetrical display of stacking boxes that all have the same x,y anchor point. Run the following program.

```
1   PImage[] boxes = new PImage[4]; //boxes[] holds 4 images
2   int build = 0; //global index variable for calling boxes[]
3   int direction = 1; //direction boxes are stacked (up/down)
4
5   PImage room; //background image
6
7   void setup() {
8   size(500,500);
9   room = loadImage("room.png");
10
11  //for loop used to load images into boxes[]
12  for (int i = 0; i< 4; i++){
13  boxes[i] = loadImage( "box" + i + ".png" );
14  }
15  }//close setup
16
17  void draw() {
18  background(255);
19  imageMode(CENTER);
20  image (room,width/2,height/2);
21
22  //"build" determines which box is displayed
23  image (boxes[build], width/2,height/2);
24
25  //"build" variable report
26  println ("build=",build);
27  } //close draw()
28
29  //change "build" whenever the mouse is pressed
30  void mousePressed(){
31  build = build + direction;
32
33  //if "build" reaches either limit of the box[] array length
34  if ((build==0) || (build==3)){
35  direction = direction * -1; //reverse its direction
36  }
37  } //close mousePressed()
```

FIGURE 8.21

TABLE 8.5   Notes on Program Example (Figure 8.21).

Location/ Code Lines	Subject	Notes
data folder	invisible image	The image box0.png is completely invisible. This was designed intentionally to delay the actual box display until the first click (since index# 0 loads when the program starts).
data folder	inactive images	The images: box4.png, box5.png are intended for use in Exercise 8.4.
11–14, data folder	**for** loop image loading	Just as we did with single image variables, we initialize images from the data folder into the **array**[] inside of **void setup**(). We could load each image as an individual line of code with the indices separated but it is more efficient to use a **for** loop. This technique works well if all the images for the **array**[] are named the same and numbered consecutively (starting at 0) in the data folder.

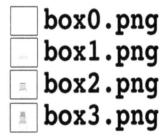

for (int i = 0; i< 4; i++){
boxes[i] = loadImage("box" + i + "png");
    }

2, 22–23, 25–26, 29–31	global index variable for the **array**[]	In this example, we want to manipulate the members of the box **array**[] individually with **mousePressed**(). A **for** loop in **void draw**() is not the solution because its index variable would be local and not accessible by the entire program. So, we create a global index variable called "build".
33–36	box build direction change	An **array**[] is said to have a "length" which starts at 0 and stops wherever the programmer specifies. In this case, our **array**[] has a length of 4: it starts with index number 0 and ends with index number 3. Within **mousePressed**(), we use a conditional statement to reverse the "direction" variable whenever "build" hits one of **array**[] ends. (See Lesson 5.6 for a review of alternating directional movement.)

Exercise 8.4

Complete the previous example (Figure 8.21), so that all 6 images labeled "box" (from the data folder) are loaded into the image **array**[] and triggered to stack up and down whenever the mouse is pressed.

FIGURE 8.22

LESSON 8.5: PLAYER OPTIONS

In Lesson 8.3, we used an **array**[] to load large variable sets simultaneously and in Lesson 8.4, we used an **array**[] to scroll through a set of images. Now, we will combine an **array**[] with keyboard movements to create a choice of cars for users to move through various screens.

FIGURE 8.23

From the download folder: "Chapter 8 Lesson Imagery", import the following images inside of a data folder:

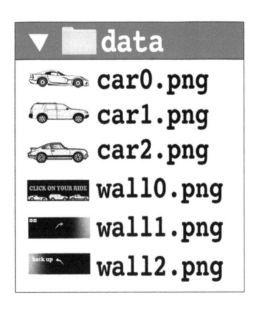

FIGURE 8.24

Now, run the following program:

```
1   //variables
2   PImage[] car = new PImage[3];   //3 cars
3   PImage[] wall = new PImage[2]; //2 backgrounds
4   int choice;   //car[] index
5   int x = 150; //x position of car[]
6   int screen = 1; //state variable for changing screens
7
8
9   void setup() {
10  size(900,300);
11
12  //load car[] images
13  for (int i = 0; i< 3; i++){
14  car[i] = loadImage ("car" + i + ".png");
15  }
16
17  //load wall[] images
18  for (int j = 0; j< 2; j++){
19  wall[j] = loadImage ("wall" + j + ".png");
20  }
21  } //close setup
22
23
24  void draw(){
25  background (255);
26  imageMode (CENTER);
27
28  //screen 1
29  if (screen == 1){
30  image(wall[0],width/2,height/2);//display 1st wall image
31
32
33  //if the 1st car region is clicked
34  if ((mousePressed)&&
35      (mouseX>0)&&(mouseX<300)&&
36      (mouseY>200)&&(mouseY<300)) {
37        choice = 0; //load 1st image into car[]
38        screen = 2; //change to next screen
39        }
40
41
42  //code continued in next figure
43
```

FIGURE 8.25   Code continued in Figure 8.26.

```
44  //or, if the 2nd car region is clicked
45  else if ((mousePressed) &&
46          (mouseX>301) && (mouseX<600) &&
47          (mouseY>200) && (mouseY<300)) {
48          choice = 1; //load 2nd image into car[]
49          screen = 2; //change to next screen
50          }
51
52  //or, if the 3rd car region is clicked
53  else if ((mousePressed) &&
54          (mouseX>601) && (mouseX<900) &&
55          (mouseY>200) && (mouseY<300)) {
56          choice = 2; //load 3rd image into car[]
57          screen = 2; //change to next screen
58          }
59  } //close screen 1
60
61  //screen 2
62  if (screen == 2) {
63  image(wall[1],width/2,height/2); //display 2nd wall image
64  image(car[choice], x,250);       //display selected car[]
65
66  if (x > 1000){ //if the car[] passes the right side,
67  screen = 3;    //then change screens
68  }
69  } //close screen 2
70
71  //screen 3
72  if (screen == 3) {
73  screen = 1; //reset to start screen
74  x = 150;    //reset car position
75  } //close screen 3
76  } //close draw
77
78
79  //move selected car[] with arrow keys
80  void keyPressed(){
81  if (keyCode == RIGHT) {
82  x += 50;
83  }
84  else if (keyCode == LEFT){
85  x -= 50;
86  }
87  }//close keyPressed
```

FIGURE 8.26

TABLE 8.6   Notes on Program Example (Figures 8.25–8.26).

Location/Code Lines	Subject	Notes
data folder	inactive image	wall2.png is intended for use in Exercise 8.5
4	**array**[] indexes	In this example, the car[] and wall[] arrays each work differently. Since, we call each image from the "wall" **array**[] in an isolated screen, we do not need a variable index. But, in the case of the "car" **array**[], we do need a global index variable because we want to be able to interchange images from the set throughout the entire program.
33–39, 44–50, 52–58	car selection	Each of these 3 code blocks activate a region of the screen that responds when the mouse is pressed. These 3 regions correspond to the 3 cars pictured in wall0.png. As soon as one of these regions is clicked, a value is assigned to the index variable "choice" and the associated car image is loaded into the "car" **array**[].
64	**array**[] selection in action	Once the index variable "choice" is initialized in "screen" 1, the selected car is controllable by keyboard movements across screens.
79–87	keyboard variations	Depending on your machine and keyboard responsiveness, the car[] reset position may vary.

Exercise 8.5

FIGURE 8.27

Build onto the previous example with the following additions:

a. Expand the "wall" **array**[] to hold all 3 wall images from the data folder.

b. Program in another "screen" (before the final reset screen) that displays wall[2] with car[choice]. This will be your new "screen" 3.

c. Program a conditional statement in this new "screen" 3 that advances to "screen" 4 when the car moves backwards off the left side.

d. Make "screen" 4 your new final reset screen.

LESSON 8.6: CHOICE-BASED PROJECTS

Now, in this final example, we will look at designing an entire interactive project as a quiz that shows the user their results. We are going to program an interactive box of candy! This strategy will combine pretty much every technique from the entire book and can serve as a template for other choice-based projects you envision.

FIGURE 8.28

From the download folder: "Chapter 8 Lesson Imagery", import the following images inside of a data folder:

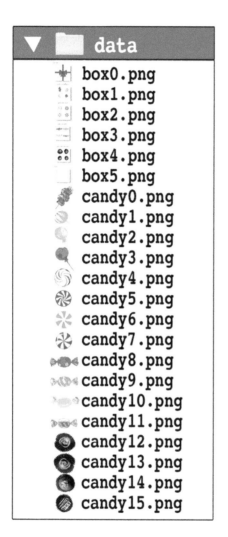

FIGURE 8.29

Now, run the following program. (Please note that the chocolate selections are not active yet.)

```
1   PImage[] candy = new PImage[16];//candy choices
2   PImage[] box = new PImage[6];    //backgrounds
3   int screen = 0;                  //screen changes
4
5   //boolean variables to track user choices
6   boolean pop1, pop2, pop3, pop4;
7   boolean mint1, mint2, mint3, mint4;
8   boolean taf1, taf2, taf3, taf4;
9
10  void setup () {
11  size (500,500);
12
13  //load images into "candy" array[]
14  for (int i = 0; i < 12; i++) {
15  candy[i] = loadImage ("candy" + i + ".png" );
16  }
17
18  //load images into "box" array[]
19  for (int j = 0; j < 6; j++) {
20  box [j] = loadImage ("box" + j + ".png" );
21  }
22  }//close setup
23
24  void draw () {
25  background (255);
26  imageMode (CENTER);
27
28  //screen 0 (start screen)
29  if (screen == 0) {
30  image (box[0], width/2, height/2);
31  } //close screen 0
32
33  //screen 1 (lollipop options screen)
34  if (screen == 1) {
35  image (box[1], width/2,height/2);
36  } //close screen 1
37
38  //screen 2 (mint options screen)
39  if (screen == 2) {
40  image (box[2], width/2, height/2);
41  } //close screen 2
42
43  //code continued in next figure
```

FIGURE 8.30 Code continued in Figures 8.31–8.34.

```
44   //screen 3 (taffy options screen)
45   if (screen == 3) {
46   image (box[3], width/2, height/2);
47   } //close screen 3
48
49   //screen 4 (chocolate options screen)
50   if (screen == 4) {
51   image (box[4], width/2, height/2);
52   } //close screen 4
53
54   //screen 5 (display candy selections screen)
55   if (screen == 5) {
56   image (box[5], width/2, height/2);
57
58   //display lollipop selection in 1st quadrant
59   if (pop1){
60   image(candy[0], 170, 160);
61   }
62   else if (pop2){
63   image(candy[1], 170, 160);
64   }
65   else if (pop3){
66   image(candy[2], 170, 160);
67   }
68   else if (pop4){
69   image(candy[3], 170, 160);
70   }
71
72   //display mint selection in 2nd quadrant
73   if (mint1){
74   image(candy[4], 320, 160);
75   }
76   else if (mint2){
77   image(candy[5], 320, 160);
78   }
79   else if (mint3){
80   image(candy[6], 320, 160);
81   }
82   else if (mint4){
83   image(candy[7], 320, 160);
84   }
85
86
87   //code continued in next figure
```

FIGURE 8.31 Code continued in Figures 8.32–8.34.

```
88    //display taffy selection in 3rd quadrant
89    if (taf1){
90    image(candy[8], 170, 310);
91    }
92    else if (taf2){
93    image(candy[9], 170, 310);
94    }
95    else if (taf3){
96    image(candy[10], 170, 310);
97    }
98    else if (taf4){
99    image(candy[11], 170, 310);
100   }
101   } //close screen 5
102
103
104   //reset to start screen
105   if (screen == 6) {
106   screen = 1;
107   pop1 = false;
108   pop2 = false;
109   pop3 = false;
110   pop4 = false;
111   mint1 = false;
112   mint2 = false;
113   mint3 = false;
114   mint4 = false;
115   taf1 = false;
116   taf2 = false;
117   taf3 = false;
118   taf4 = false;
119   } //close screen 6
120
121
122   //variable reports
123   println ("mouseX=",mouseX, "mouseY=",mouseY);
124   println ("screen=",screen);
125
126   } //close draw
127
128
129   //code continued in next figure
130
131
```

FIGURE 8.32   Code continued in Figures 8.33–8.34.

```
132  //press mouse to change screens & activate candy choices
133  void mousePressed() {
134  screen = screen + 1;
135
136  //click on your preferred lollipop region
137  if (screen == 2){
138  if ((mouseX>75)&&(mouseX<250)&&(mouseY>75)&&(mouseY<250)){
139  pop1 = true;
140  }
141  else if
142  ((mouseX>250)&&(mouseX<425)&&(mouseY>75)&&(mouseY<250)){
143  pop2 = true;
144  }
145  else if
146  ((mouseX>75)&&(mouseX<250)&&(mouseY>250)&&(mouseY<400)){
147  pop3 = true;
148  }
149  else if
150  ((mouseX>250)&&(mouseX<425)&&(mouseY>250)&&(mouseY<400)){
151  pop4 = true;
152  }
153  }//close lollipop options
154
155
156  //click on your preferred mint region
157  if (screen== 3){
158  if ((mouseX>75)&&(mouseX<250)&&(mouseY>75)&&(mouseY<250)){
159  mint1 = true;
160  }
161  else if
162  ((mouseX>250)&&(mouseX<425)&&(mouseY>75)&&(mouseY<250)){
163  mint2 = true;
164  }
165  else if
166  ((mouseX>75)&&(mouseX<250)&&(mouseY>250)&&(mouseY<400)){
167  mint3 = true;
168  }
169  else if
170  ((mouseX>250)&&(mouseX<425)&&(mouseY> 250)&&(mouseY<400)){
171  mint4 = true;
172  }
173  } //close mint options
174
175  //code continued in next figure
```

FIGURE 8.33 Code continued in Figure 8.34.

```
176  //click on your preferred taffy region
177  if (screen == 4) {
178  if ((mouseX>75)&&(mouseX<250)&&(mouseY>75)&&(mouseY<250)){
179  taf1 = true;
180  }
181  else if
182  ((mouseX>250)&&(mouseX<425)&&(mouseY>75)&&(mouseY<250)){
183  taf2 = true;
184  }
185  else if
186  ((mouseX>75)&&(mouseX<250)&&(mouseY>250)&&(mouseY<400)){
187  taf3 = true;
188  }
189  else if
190  ((mouseX>250)&&(mouseX<425)&&(mouseY> 250)&&(mouseY<400)){
191  taf4 = true;
192  }
193  } //close taffy options
194  } //close mousePressed
```

FIGURE 8.34

TABLE 8.7   Notes on Program Example (Figures 8.30–8.34).

Location/ Code Lines	Subject	Notes
data folder	inactive images	The images: candy12.png, candy13.png, candy14.png, and candy15.png are intended for use in Exercise 8.6
5–8	**boolean** variables	In this example, we use **boolean** variables to create toggle switches that register which candies are selected by the user. As an aside, it is possible to write a **boolean array**[]. But, in this code example, the organization of the program reads clearer with individual **boolean** variables. Also, please note the groups of 4 boolean variables declared on one line. This syntax was implemented to remove clutter and does not change variable functioning. You can apply this to **int** and **float** variables as well.
3, 132–134	screen changes	The state variable "screen" advances each candy box scene by 1 with **mousePressed**().
33–52, 136–193	making selections	In screens 1–4, candy selections are logged based on where the mouse is pressed. (Remember, the chocolate selections are not yet active.) Each **mousePressed**() achieves two purposes: advance the screen levels and register the user's candy choices. Choices are saved as **true boolean** variables.
		Also, when looking at the candy choice conditionals in **mousePressed**(), you might think that the "screen" variable value should match the candy section displayed. For example, since lollipops are displayed in "screen" 1, the conditional should reflect this. However, in line 137, we see that the "screen" variable is actually 2 for the lollipop selection. This is because as soon as you click a choice you are also simultaneously advancing to the next value of "screen".
54–101, 132–194	selection results	Once "screen" becomes 5, conditional tests for pops, mints, and taffies are checked to see which **boolean** variables turned **true** for display in the candy box.
104–119	reset	When we click to begin the experience again, we reset the start screen and all of the candy choices. So, "screen" becomes 1 and every boolean is returned to **false**.

Exercise 8.6

Complete the previous example so that the chocolate selection works as well.

FIGURE 8.35

CONCLUSION

We are now at the drop off point from guided instruction to independent creative application. There are many ways to head into your final project. You can remix one of the examples from this chapter or start with one of the project examples in the download folder. The key is to start with a project plan and begin coding with an overall structure. Then add things in piece by piece to test their impact on the rest of the program. It is also a good idea to prioritize what challenges you will tackle first, here's a few final tips before you begin.

- Remember to always check your bracket positioning. Small adjustments of bracket syntax will make huge differences in the functionality of your code.

- Use **println()** to verify your variables are doing what you want them to.

- When you experiment with your project, save multiple versions of the same program. As I wrote in the introduction, sometimes a pursuit may take you down a rabbit hole and cause you to forget where you were before you started testing new ideas. To avoid this, keep a copy of your first solution attempt off to the side while you run new tests on other versions.

- Take a break! Solutions will come to you when you rest and take your mind off a frustrating code problem.

- If all else fails, consider using the Processing forum (https://discourse. processing.org). It is free to sign-up and you will find a wealth of programmers including college students that enjoy looking at code challenges and helping new learners. The generosity of these members is incredible and these boards are moderated, so rest assured that this is a safe space for programmers! Your success at receiving useful help from the forum depends on how you engage with it. Before posting, do a keyword search of previous posts. The answer might be waiting for you without having to wait for an answer. If you do post, always read the forum's guidelines before asking questions. When you follow the guidelines you will get great results.

- In many ways, this book just scratches the surface of what you can do with Processing. If you would like to implement coding techniques not presented in this text, there is no end to the amount of resources available to you. From books to free tutorial websites and YouTube videos – you will have a wealth of information to explore.

Onwards to your masterpiece!

FINAL PROJECT: MULTILEVEL INTERACTIVE EXPERIENCE

Create a visually dynamic and interactively interesting project with multiple screen changes. This could be a game, simulation, story, quiz, or animated art experience. See project examples in the downloads folder for Chapter 8, available from the publisher's website.

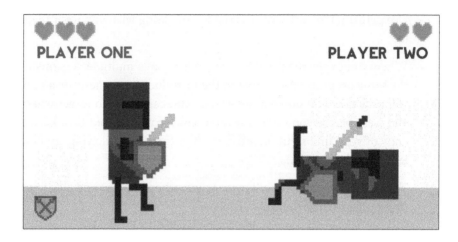

FIGURE 8.36 Student project example: two player, knight fighting game. (Printed with permission from Blake Brownyard.)

FIGURE 8.37 Student project example: two player, knight fighting game. (Printed with permission from Blake Brownyard.)

FIGURE 8.38   Student project example: interactive visual metaphor about bias and the "other". (Printed with permission from Maiah Cooper.)

FIGURE 8.39   Student project example: interactive visual metaphor about bias and the "other". (Printed with permission from Maiah Cooper.)

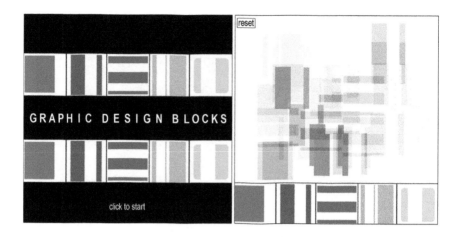

FIGURE 8.40   Project example: graphic design sketch pad.

Index

Italicized and **bold** pages refer to figures and tables respectively.

D

E